CREATE YOUR CALLING

WHY GOD WANTS YOU TO START A BUSINESS AND HOW TO STEP INTO IT

PENNY RAY

MEANSCRIBE PRODUCTIONS

Create Your Calling: *Why God Wants You to Start a Business and How to Step Into It*

Copyright © 2025 by Penny Ray

Limit of Liability/Disclaimer: While the author has made every effort to provide accurate and up-to-date information in this book, he makes no representations or warranties with respect to the accuracy or completeness of its contents. The advice and strategies contained herein may not be suitable for every situation. This work is sold with the understanding that the author is not engaged in rendering legal, accounting, or other professional services. If professional assistance is required, the services of a competent professional should be sought. The author shall not be liable for any loss of profit or any other commercial damages, including but not limited to special, incidental, consequential, or other damages.

Scripture quotations are taken from the King James Version of the Bible, which is in the public domain.

ISBN: 979-8-218-85409-6

For additional resources, visit www.CreateYourCallingNow.com

First Edition

DEDICATION

To my father, without whom I would likely be dead.

To my mother, who gave me life, showed me love, and taught me faith.

And to future generations, who will build something beautiful with the gifts God has given them.

ACKNOWLEDGMENTS

To the men of my first-ever men's group: Ed Hawks, George Dukin, James Williams, Joey Reid, John Christensen, Levi Killian, and William Joines. When I walked into that room for the first time, I had no idea how much your fellowship would change my life. You've given me a safe place to think out loud, wrestle with big questions, and share the messy parts of my journey. Through your stories, your wisdom, and your willingness to listen to mine, you've helped me understand Christ and His calling on my life in ways I never expected. This book exists partly because you showed me what it looks like when men encourage each other to step boldly into God's purposes. Thank you for being iron that sharpens iron.

Contents

INTRODUCTION

There's no shortage of business advice in the world. The internet is full of entrepreneurs showing off their success—the cars, the vacations, the freedom to work from anywhere. Don't get me wrong—there's nothing sinful about nice things. God created material blessings for us to enjoy. But if that's your only reason for starting a business, you're missing the bigger picture.

I believe God created business for a much deeper purpose than just making you rich. Think about it: every successful business solves a problem for someone. Every service makes someone's life better. Every product meets a genuine need. When you really serve people well, they pay you for that value.

That's not an accident. That's God's design.

He created business as a way for His children to serve each other. When you start a business, you're not just trying to make money—you're participating in God's plan for people to work together, solve problems, and take care of each other.

Your community needs the solution you've been thinking about. Your family needs the provision and flexibility that business ownership can provide. Your church needs the resources you'll be able to give when your business succeeds.

The money you earn isn't just profit. It's proof that you served someone well.

Most business coaches tell you to "find your why" before you start. That's fine advice, but I think there's something more important: understanding God's "why" for business in the first place.

Your personal why might be about providing for your family, gaining freedom, or building wealth. Those are good motivations. But God's why is about using the unique gifts He gave you to serve others and advance His kingdom through the marketplace.

Here's what I've learned: the faster you align your business with God's purposes, the more successful you'll become. Not just financially, but in ways that actually matter.

"For I know the thoughts that I think toward you, saith the Lord, thoughts of peace, and not of evil, to give you an expected end." (Jeremiah 29:11, KJV)

God has good plans for you, and those plans include using your gifts productively.

The problem is, too many Christians are hiding their gifts behind fear. They're worried they're not qualified enough, smart enough, or experienced enough to start something meaningful.

That's fear talking, and fear isn't from God.

If God gave you the gifts, He expects you to use them. If He placed a burden on your heart for certain people or problems, He wants you to do something about it.

Your struggles have prepared you for something. Your experiences have equipped you for a purpose. Your gifts are meant to be used, not buried.

When you step out in faith and start building something that serves others, God moves with you.

That's what this book is about: helping you discover what God is calling you to build and giving you the practical steps to build it well.

The question isn't whether God wants you in business. The question is: which business is He calling you to build? Not every business idea is a God idea. Not every opportunity is an open door. And not every entrepreneurial impulse is a calling to create.

1

THE BLUEPRINT I NEVER HAD

Why this book had to be written

For a long time, I struggled to understand my father's choices. Don't get me wrong—I'm grateful for what he provided. The situation was complicated from the start.

My father had two children before me from another relationship. When he got my mom pregnant, he was also involved with another woman who gave birth to one of my half-sisters just three months after I was born. He had options—he could have chosen to be with the other woman, or neither of them. But he chose to marry my mom. They stayed together for 28 years.

When we were stationed in Germany, he extended his tour multiple times so I could finish high school there instead of returning to crime-ridden DC during the height of the crack cocaine epidemic. That decision probably saved my life.

He was present. He kept me out of jail. For that, I cannot thank him enough.

But as I got older, I realized something was missing from what I'd learned about being a man.

My father had chosen a career in government and, to my knowledge, had never built anything of his own. He used to talk about owning a grocery store one day, but he never did it. Over the years, he had children from multiple relationships—I knew of two older than me, and learned as I got older that there were others younger than me as well. He was supporting our household and paying child support on a government salary—money that came from taxpayers, not from anything he had created or built.

Let me be clear about something: I have no problem with public service. In fact, I served in the military myself for four years, though that was because my father pushed me in that direction rather than my own choice.

But I don't believe anyone should spend their entire working life living off taxpayer-funded paychecks. I'm not trying to hurt feelings here, but public service should actually be service—a season where you gain experience and serve others, then take that knowledge and build something that honors God, creates value and serves people without depending on tax dollars.

There are several reasons why I feel this way. For starters, government jobs are funded by taxes collected from private sector workers and businesses. The more people who depend on government paychecks, the fewer people there are creating the wealth that funds those paychecks. Taxpayer-funded service should be a relatively short-term commitment. The skills you develop, the connections you make, the problems you learn to solve—that should all become fuel for building something in the private sector, not an excuse to stay on the government payroll for thirty years.

Beyond the practical limitations, working for the government for decades comes with strings attached that can compromise your ability to stand boldly for Christ. When your livelihood depends on a government paycheck, you're put in a position where you might have to choose between obeying God and keeping your job.

The apostles faced pressure from authorities to stop preaching, and Peter's response in Acts 5:29 should guide every believer: "We ought to obey God rather than men." But how can you boldly stand for biblical truth when standing might cost you your career and your family's provision? Building your own business gives you the freedom to obey God rather than men without fearing economic consequences.

There's an even deeper concern: when you depend on government employment for decades, you risk prioritizing the state's interests over your family's wellbeing. Your schedule, your location, your financial security—all controlled by bureaucratic decisions rather than what's best for the people you love most. God designed the family unit as the foundational building block of society, not the state. When government employment requires you to put the state's needs consistently ahead of your family's, that's a reversal of God's design.

More fundamentally, staying in a government position for your entire working life limits your growth in ways that may prevent you from living up to the potential God gave you. The parable of the talents makes this clear: "For unto every one that hath shall be given, and he shall have abundance: but from him that hath not shall be taken away even that which he hath." (Matthew 25:29, KJV)

Each of us has talents given by God that need to be nurtured and developed to reach their full potential. In my experience, government positions are more likely to stifle those God-given talents than develop them. When you limit your development to only what the government wants you to do in your specific role, you're not multiplying the gifts God gave you—you're burying them. Your growth becomes constrained by bureaucratic boundaries instead of being unleashed by divine purpose.

Now, someone might say, "If no one spent 30 years in the military, we wouldn't have any generals." That's only true because of how the current system is structured, not because it's the only way it could work.

History shows us that some of the most effective military leaders—Napoleon, Civil War generals, World War II commanders—reached high command in their twenties and thirties when circumstances demanded it.

More importantly, if someone truly feels called by God to military leadership at the highest levels, that calling would likely be evident from the beginning through the officer track, not after decades as enlisted personnel. If God has called you to strategic military leadership, that's between you and Him. But for most people, extended government service becomes a comfortable trap.

What I'm addressing is the security mindset—and this applies whether you're in the military or working as a civil servant for 30 years to secure a government pension. Whether you're a town clerk, school system employee, or any other government worker who's chosen security over calling, the principle is the same.

When you enlist in the military, you're essentially telling the government: "You can tell me where to live, what to do, who my friends can be, what clothes to wear, and how to spend my time." You submit your life to their authority for decades.

The same thing happens with long-term civil service—you submit your potential, your gifts, and your time to a system that limits your growth in exchange for the promise of security.

But here's what I believe: we should be enlisting in the service of God, not man. We ought to obey God rather than men. When you give your life to government service for 30 years, you're submitting to human authority instead of divine calling.

God doesn't want you dependent on a system that can change its rules, cut your benefits, or eliminate your position. He wants you free to serve Him fully, using all the gifts He's given you to build something meaningful.

When you build your own business in alignment with God and rely on His provision instead of taxpayer-funded paychecks, you don't have to worry about being furloughed during government shutdowns or having your benefits suspended when politicians can't agree on a budget. You're depending on God's faithfulness rather than man's systems, and His provision doesn't get caught up in political gridlock.

What frustrated me most about my father's career choice wasn't the service itself, but what it meant for my own development. I had been drawn to start something of my own my entire life, but I had no blueprint from him. No model of what it looked like for a man to build something from nothing. No understanding of how to create value, serve others, and generate wealth through enterprise instead of depending on a government paycheck.

For years, I carried anger inside me that I couldn't fully explain. It wasn't the kind of anger that exploded in arguments or caused me to lash out at people. It was a quiet, persistent frustration that gnawed at me every day. Even when I was good at my job—even when I became a journalist and knew I was supposed to be telling stories—I felt like I wasn't doing what I was meant to do with my life.

I felt stuck. Not because I didn't have options, but because none of the options felt right. I was mad when things wouldn't go my way, mad when opportunities didn't materialize, mad when I couldn't see a clear path forward.

What I knew was that I had skills and abilities that weren't being fully used. I felt like a slave to a world that wanted to keep me in a box, doing just enough to get by but never enough to truly thrive. I believed I could shape my reality, but I didn't have the knowledge of how to do it and hadn't yet learned the difference between my will and God's.

It wasn't until I reconnected with God that I began to see more clearly. What I had interpreted as being stuck was actually preparation. What felt like wasted time was actually skill-building. What seemed like random experiences were actually pieces of a larger puzzle that God was putting together.

What I Learned Too Late

Here's something I wish I'd understood earlier: both manhood and womanhood are learned lifestyles. They're not automatic. They're transferred through modeling, teaching, and skill-building from the adults in your life.

You learn how to be a man by watching other men live it out. You absorb it through conversations and guidance from men who've walked the path before you. You develop the skills through practice and application of what you've observed.

The same is true for women—they learn womanhood from watching other women navigate relationships, motherhood, and their roles in building families and communities. But fathers also play a crucial role in shaping their daughters' understanding of what godly womanhood looks like and what they should expect from men. Without a father who models what it means to build and provide, daughters may not recognize these qualities as essential in a partner, leading them to settle for men who aren't prepared to be the leaders and providers God designed them to be.

When that lifestyle transfer is incomplete or missing—whether it's sons not learning from fathers or daughters not seeing healthy examples from either parent—it creates gaps that can hold both people back in their relationships and their individual callings.

Now, I'm not saying a man who works for someone else is not ready for marriage. But I am saying this: when two become one in marriage, as God designed, you need a blueprint for building your life together that isn't dependent on the government or any employer's whims.

I've been fired, laid off, or let go involuntarily at least seven times that I can think of. If you're building your marriage on the foundation of employer dependence with no plan for what happens when that job disappears, you're setting yourself up for disaster. Financial stress is one of the leading causes of divorce, and it's hard to become truly "one" with your spouse when you're both working separate jobs with separate schedules, building separate parts of your lives.

When you build a business together—or at least build your life around a shared vision rather than separate employers—you have a reason to plan together, work together, and spend more time together than just the hours outside of work. Man and woman must be one with God and each other, with a plan they can adapt together as circumstances change. That's hard to do when your livelihood depends entirely on decisions made by people who don't care about your marriage.

From my perspective as a child looking up at my father, I saw someone who was more focused on consumption than creation. He loved throwing parties, making daiquiris, having people over to socialize. There's nothing wrong with enjoying life, but that seemed to be all he wanted to do. Even now, when we talk, it's usually about some party he's planning or vacation he's taking, not about building or creating something meaningful.

What I was missing was a model of what it looked like to build something together as a family. To create value. To work toward a vision that was bigger than just getting by.

The Cost of Just Surviving

Looking back, I can see that my parents weren't building together—they were just surviving. And when you're fighting for survival, it's hard to love someone else the way you're designed to.

This is especially true for women. A woman can't fully love and respect a man when she doesn't trust that he'll get them through whatever troubles they're facing. When she's worried they won't make it and believes he won't pull his weight, when she doesn't see him as the warrior she needs him to be, the relationship suffers. It's not her fault. It's not his fault. It's just the reality of what happens when people are stuck in survival mode instead of building mode.

My parents had four kids living at home—me, my brother who is three years younger, my adopted sister who is also three years younger, and my youngest sister who is about ten years younger than me. My father also had children from other relationships, including some younger than me, which I learned about as I got older.

From what I could see, we definitely weren't rich, despite the occasional new car or the nice quarters we lived in. My parents liked having things that looked impressive—German Schranks, grandfather clocks, glass tables—the kind of material things that make it appear we had money. But those things can be financed to the hilt. You can look like you're doing well while being extended to zero every month, making payments on everything for the rest of your life.

I don't know my father's exact financial situation, and I want to be fair about that. But what I do know is that we could have been building wealth instead of just managing expenses. We could have been creating something that would benefit not just our immediate family, but future generations.

To my knowledge, no such assets exist. I'm sure my parents have life insurance policies, but that's not the same as building generational wealth. I've never heard of my father creating a job or business opportunity for any of his 12 children—whether as a stepping stone out of high school, a way to work through college, or help during tough times.

In all my years growing up and even now as an adult, I've never had a conversation with my father about a business he's building or has built. He's mentioned that he wants to do this or that, but I've never seen any of those ideas come to fruition. He may own stocks or be invested in someone else's venture. But as far as creating something that generates opportunities and wealth for future generations of our family, I haven't seen it.

When we do talk, he doesn't talk about building anything. He talks about parties, vacations, and enjoying life. And there's nothing wrong with enjoying life—but when that's all there is, when there's no blueprint being created and no foundation being built for future generations, that's the real cost of just surviving instead of building.

The Generational Impact

As of this writing, I am single with no children. I believe this is partly because I watched my father have numerous children from multiple relationships without the financial foundation to give all of them the opportunities they deserved. I saw the strain it put on our household and decided I wouldn't follow that pattern.

I determined early on that I wouldn't have children unless I could build something substantial enough to provide for them properly. Not just survive, but thrive. Not just pay bills, but create opportunities.

But here's the problem: I had no blueprint for how to do that.

When I finally decided to start building something of my own, I had to turn to strangers. I had to buy courses from people I'd never met. I had to piece together knowledge from books, seminars, and trial and error because I'd never seen it modeled at home.

This book exists because I don't want you to struggle the same way I did.

Why This Matters for Your Business

If you're reading this book, you feel called to build something. That calling isn't an accident. God placed it in you for a reason.

But maybe, like me, you don't have a clear blueprint for how to do it. Maybe you grew up in a household where people worked for others but never built anything of their own. Maybe you've been trying to figure it out through courses and books and advice from strangers.

That's okay. That's actually part of your story.

The gaps in your foundation don't disqualify you from building something meaningful. They just mean you have to be more intentional about filling those gaps with the right knowledge, the right mentors, and most importantly, the right perspective on why you're building in the first place.

That foundation isn't just practical—it's spiritual. It's understanding that your business isn't just about making money. It's about stewardship. It's about using the gifts God gave you to serve others and create value in the world. It's about building something that honors Him and provides for the people you love.

It's about breaking cycles and creating new patterns for the generations that come after you.

The Guide You Need

My father may not appreciate this story being told, but I've learned that you can't build something new until you're honest about what came before. This truth is part of what drives me to help others build differently.

I'm sharing my story because I want you to understand that the struggles you've faced, the gaps in your knowledge, the lack of mentorship—none of that disqualifies you from building something meaningful. In fact, it might be exactly what qualifies you to build something different. Something better.

Maybe the struggles I went through, the courses I bought, the mistakes I made, the businesses I started and failed at and eventually succeeded with—maybe all of that was preparation for helping you avoid the same struggles.

Maybe God allowed me to figure it out the hard way so I could give you an easier path.

That's what the following chapters are about. Not just how to choose a business, but how to build it on the right foundation. How to make sure you're creating something that serves God, serves others, and creates the kind of legacy you want to leave behind.

You don't have to figure this out alone. You don't have to buy course after course from strangers who don't know your story or your calling.

You have a Father in heaven who wants to partner with you in building something beautiful. And you have this book, which is the guide I wish I'd had when I was starting out.

Let's build something together.

2

THE FAITH FOUNDATION

Before you pick the business, know Who you're building it with

I had it all figured out. At least, that's what I told myself as I scrolled through another real estate investing course at 2am. The sales page promised everything I wanted: financial freedom, passive income, and the ability to make money without using my own capital.

I'd already bought similar courses in the past. Each one promised to be different. Each one taught me something, but I never fully put them into practice.

But this time felt different. This guru had testimonials. Screenshots of success stories. A compelling narrative about going from broke to millionaire through creative real estate strategies.

I pulled out my credit card. Again.

Three months later, I was more confused than ever and starting to wonder if entrepreneurship was even for me. Some of the strategies felt questionable—requiring me to hold back information that might affect people's willingness to work with me. Every time I tried to implement what I'd learned, something inside me recoiled.

I was chasing success, but I'd forgotten to ask the most important question: Who was I building this with?

Calling vs. Chasing

There's a massive difference between being called to build something and simply chasing the next opportunity.

When you're chasing, you're reacting. Reacting to pressure from family who think you should be making more money. Reacting to fear that you're falling behind your peers. Reacting to the latest success story on social media that makes your current situation look pathetic by comparison.

When you're called, you're responding. Responding to a burden God has placed on your heart. Responding to a problem you can't ignore. Responding to a vision that won't leave you alone, even when it would be easier to stay where you are.

The difference shows up in everything. Your motivation. Your methods. Your ability to persist when things get hard.

Chase-driven entrepreneurs burn out because their fuel source is external. They need constant validation, constant progress, constant proof that they're on the right track. When the validation stops coming, they quit.

Called entrepreneurs endure because their fuel source is internal and eternal. They know why they're building what they're building, and that "why" doesn't depend on immediate results or other people's approval.

But here's what most people don't understand about calling: it's not always dramatic.

You don't need a burning bush or an audible voice from heaven. Sometimes calling looks like a persistent burden for a specific group of people. Sometimes it's a skill you can't stop thinking about developing. Sometimes it's a problem that keeps you up at night because you can see the solution so clearly.

There's another aspect of calling that's equally important: the character you show when circumstances force you to make a choice. Abraham's story illustrates this perfectly.

The Abraham Principle: When Faith Overrides Fear

Abraham was one of the wealthiest men of his time. He had herds, silver, gold, and influence. But even blessings can create tension.

As Abraham and his nephew Lot prospered, their herds grew so large that the land couldn't support them both. Soon, their herdsmen were clashing over grazing rights, turning family into competitors.

Abraham had every cultural right to claim the best land. He was older. He was the leader. He was the one God had called. In that culture, age and authority meant everything. Lot should have deferred to him.

But instead of fighting for position, Abraham did something shocking:

"Let there be no strife, I pray thee, between me and thee, and between my herdmen and thy herdmen; for we be brethren. Is not the whole land before thee? separate thyself, I pray thee, from me: if thou wilt take the left hand, then I will go to the right; or if thou depart to the right hand, then I will go to the left." (Genesis 13:8-9, KJV)

Lot immediately chose the lush, fertile Jordan Valley. The "obvious" best business decision. The land that looked most profitable, most promising, most likely to generate quick returns.

Abraham was left with rocky hills and less promising ground.

Every business guru would have told Abraham he'd just made a massive mistake. He'd given up his competitive advantage. He'd let emotion override strategy.

But here's the twist: Lot's short-term gain led him straight into Sodom, a city destined for destruction. His "smart" business decision put him in the path of judgment.

Abraham's act of faith, meanwhile, triggered something unexpected. Right after Lot made his choice, God spoke to Abraham again:

"Lift up now thine eyes, and look from the place where thou art northward, and southward, and eastward, and westward: For all the land which thou seest, to thee will I give it, and to thy seed for ever." (Genesis 13:14-15, KJV)

Abraham's surrender didn't lead to loss. It led to a reaffirmation of God's promise that his descendants would inherit not just a good pasture, but nations.

This is the Abraham Principle: everything that happens in your business journey happens for a reason, and God can use even apparent setbacks to position you for His greater plan.

Abraham didn't surrender his rights; he chose faith over fear, trusting that God's provision was bigger than what he could see in the moment. When you trust God's provision, you don't have to grasp for control, manipulate circumstances, or fight for what you think you deserve. What He intends for you cannot be taken by anyone else.

This doesn't mean you become passive or stop working hard. Abraham continued to build his wealth and expand his influence. But he did so with confidence in God's promises rather than anxiety about missing out.

Stewardship Over Hype

There's a common misconception that being meek means being weak or passive. But when Jesus said "Blessed are the meek: for they shall inherit the earth" (Matthew 5:5, KJV), the Greek word used in the New Testament to record His teaching—praus (πραΰς)—actually refers to controlled strength, not weakness. It's the same word used in ancient Greek to describe a powerful warhorse that has been trained to respond to its rider's guidance. The horse hasn't lost its strength or power—it has learned to channel that strength under direction.

Biblical meekness is about having the strength to build something significant but choosing to submit that strength to God's guidance rather than your own ego or ambition. It's controlled power, not powerlessness.

This brings us to a fundamental question that every faith-driven entrepreneur must answer: What can I build that I can faithfully manage?

Notice I didn't ask what you can build that will make you rich, famous, or impressive to others. I asked what you can build that you can faithfully manage.

Stewardship is about more than just handling money well. It's about recognizing that everything you have, every skill you've developed, every opportunity that comes your way, belongs to God first. You're the manager, not the owner.

This perspective changes everything about how you approach business.

Instead of asking, "What's the fastest way to make money?" you ask, "What has God equipped me to manage well?"

Instead of asking, "What's trending right now?" you ask, "What burden has He placed on my heart that won't go away?"

Instead of asking, "What will make me look successful?" you ask, "What can I build that will serve others and honor Him?"

I learned this lesson the expensive way. After spending thousands of dollars on real estate courses with nothing to show for it, I finally stopped chasing other people's strategies and started asking different questions. What was I actually good at? What problems did I care about solving? What could I build that aligned with my values instead of violating them?

The answers led me to start a marketing agency helping established businesses tell their stories better. Not as flashy as the "make money in real estate with no money down" promise, but sustainable, meaningful, and completely aligned with the skills God had been developing in me through radio, journalism, and screenwriting.

Today, I have clients who genuinely appreciate my help, and I sleep well at night knowing my business serves people instead of just serving my ego. Plus, it's positioning me to eventually build the film production company I've been dreaming about for years.

Your Unique Design

I can't remember exactly where I first heard this concept, but I know multiple sermons have been based on the scientific fact that salt and light are change agents by definition. Scientifically, salt changes whatever it comes into contact with through preservation, flavor enhancement, and chemical reactions. Light changes environments by illuminating darkness, enabling growth, and revealing what was hidden.

Here's what's remarkable: our bodies are made of both salt (sodium and chloride are essential to our cellular function) and light (our cells actually emit biophotons). If we're literally composed of change agents, doesn't that suggest we're designed to be change agents ourselves?

This is exactly what Jesus meant when He said, "Ye are the salt of the earth... Ye are the light of the world" (Matthew 5:13-14, KJV). And it's what Paul was getting at in Romans 12:2: "And be not conformed to this world: but be ye transformed by the renewing of your mind, that ye may prove what is that good, and acceptable, and perfect, will of God."

You're not designed to conform to existing business blueprints or accept the status quo. You're designed to be a change agent—to find ways to make services better, products more effective, and customer experiences more meaningful. Even if you start with a concept similar to what others are doing, your role is to transform it, improve it, and make it uniquely yours.

God didn't mass-produce entrepreneurs. He custom-designed each one for a specific purpose.

Your personality, your background, your experiences, even your struggles have all been preparing you for something specific. The business you're called to build will be uniquely suited to who you are and what you've been through.

This is why copying someone else's exact approach rarely works. You're not them. You don't have their personality, their network, their skills, or their calling. What works for them might be completely wrong for you.

Instead of recreating someone else's business, uncover the way you're wired and build from that.

Start by asking these questions:

What energizes you? Not what you think should energize you, but what actually does. What activities make you lose track of time? What conversations light you up? What problems do you find yourself thinking about even when you're supposed to be relaxing?

What breaks your heart? What injustices make you angry? What needs do you see that others seem to ignore? Often, your calling is hidden in your compassion.

What has your pain taught you? Your struggles aren't wasted if they prepare you to help others facing similar challenges. Some of the most powerful businesses are built by people who solved their own problems first, then realized others needed the same solution.

What do people consistently ask for your help with? Sometimes others see your gifts more clearly than you do. Pay attention to the requests that keep coming your way.

Your unique design isn't an accident. It's preparation for the work God has called you to do.

Biblical Entrepreneurs

Here's what many Christians don't realize: the Bible is packed with entrepreneurs.

Not just people who happened to do business on the side, but serious, strategic, wealth-building business owners who understood markets, managed employees, and built enterprises that lasted for generations.

Take the Proverbs 31 woman. Most sermons focus on her character, but look closer at what she actually did for work. She wasn't just managing a household. She was running a diversified business empire.

"She considereth a field, and buyeth it: with the fruit of her hands she planteth a vineyard... She maketh fine linen, and selleth it; and delivereth girdles unto the merchant." (Proverbs 31:16, 24, KJV)

This woman understood real estate investment, agricultural development, manufacturing, and wholesale distribution. She had multiple revenue streams, reinvested her profits, and built relationships with other business owners. Her success didn't compete with her family life. It enhanced it.

Then there's Lydia, who dealt in purple cloth. This wasn't some small craft business. Purple dye was one of the most expensive commodities in the ancient world. Lydia was operating at the luxury end of the market, which meant she had significant capital, sophisticated supply chains, and high-end clientele.

When Paul met her in Philippi, she was successful enough to own a home large enough to host traveling missionaries. Her business became a platform for ministry, not an obstacle to it.

And don't forget the parable of the talents. Jesus told a story where the master commended the servants who invested and doubled his money. The one who buried his talent out of fear? He got rebuked.

The message is clear: God expects us to multiply what He's given us, not just preserve it.

These aren't random examples. They're patterns that reveal God's heart for His people to be productive, creative, and generous with the resources He provides.

But here's what's crucial about every one of these biblical entrepreneurs: their businesses aligned with their values and served their larger purpose. They weren't just chasing money. They were building something that fit into God's bigger plan for their lives.

The Proverbs 31 woman's business strengthened her family. Lydia's success created a base for ministry. The faithful servants in the parable were rewarded because they stewarded well what belonged to their master.

That's the blueprint. Build something profitable, but build it with purpose. Create wealth, but create it in a way that serves others and honors God.

Your business can do the same thing. But first, you need to know what you're actually called to build.

The Foundation Question

Before you choose what business to start, you need to answer this foundational question: Are you building with God or just asking Him to bless what you've already decided to do?

There's a huge difference.

When you build with God, you start with prayer, move forward with wisdom, and hold your plans loosely enough that He can redirect them when necessary. You're genuinely open to His guidance, even when it doesn't match your original vision.

When you just ask God to bless your predetermined plans, you've already made up your mind. You want His endorsement, not His direction. You'll pray for success, but you won't pause to ask if you're pursuing the right thing in the first place.

Building with God requires humility. It means admitting you don't have all the answers. It means being willing to wait for clarity instead of rushing ahead with the first idea that excites you. It means choosing faithfulness over flashiness, sustainability over speed.

But here's what you get in return: peace in the process, wisdom for decisions, and the confidence that comes from knowing you're not building alone.

The question isn't whether God wants you in business. The question is: which business is He calling you to build?

That's what we'll figure out in the next chapter.

But first, you need to settle this foundation issue. Are you ready to build with Him, or are you just looking for His stamp of approval on your own plans?

Your answer to that question will determine everything that follows.

3

THE CLARITY FILTER

4 God-honoring questions to choose the right business

I had been staring at the whiteboard in my home office for two hours. On the left side, I'd written "BUSINESS IDEAS" in blue marker. Underneath, a list that kept growing: writing coach, freelance writing, laundromat owner, marketing agency, vending machine route, film production company, real estate investing.

On the right side, I'd written "PROS & CONS" and started analyzing each option. Market size. Startup costs. Competition levels. Profit margins.

The more I analyzed, the more confused I became.

Every business idea had potential. Every one also had significant drawbacks. The marketing agency required constant client management. The film production company needed massive upfront capital. The coaching felt too dependent on my personal time.

By hour three, I had added "PRAYER" to the top of the whiteboard and was asking God to just tell me which one to pick.

But what if I was asking the wrong question?

What if instead of asking God to choose from my list, I needed to ask God to help me understand what He'd been preparing me for all along?

The Problem with Most Business Selection

Here's how most people choose a business: they start with what's working for other people, then try to figure out if they can make it work for themselves.

They see someone making money with real estate, so they think about getting into real estate. They hear about a friend's successful consulting practice, so they consider consulting. They read about someone's six-figure online course business, so they start planning their own course.

This approach has three major problems.

First, you're always playing catch-up. By the time you hear about someone else's success, the market has usually shifted. What worked for them two years ago might not work for you today.

Second, you're building on someone else's foundation instead of your own. Their success was built on their unique combination of skills, connections, timing, and calling. Trying to replicate their results without their foundation is like trying to build the second floor of a house without the first floor.

Third, you're starting with the wrong question. Instead of asking "What business should I start?" you're asking "Which successful business can I copy?"

There's a better way.

The Clarity Filter Approach

What if instead of starting with business models, you started with three fundamental questions that help you understand what God has equipped you to build?

What if instead of looking at what's working for others, you looked at what He's been preparing in you?

What if instead of trying to fit yourself into someone else's success story, you discovered the unique story He wants to write through your business?

That's what the Clarity Filter is about. Four questions that cut through the noise and get to the heart of what you're actually called to build:

1. SKILL – What are you good at or excited to learn?

2. SERVICE – Who do you feel called to serve?

3. SUSTAINABILITY – Can this model support your desired life?

4. SEASON – What season of life are you in right now?

These aren't just practical questions. They're spiritual ones. Each one is designed to help you align your business with how God has wired you, what He's placed on your heart, and the life He's calling you to live.

Let me show you how this worked in my own journey.

Question 1: SKILL – What are you good at or excited to learn?

When I was in my twenties, I thought I wanted to be in television. I didn't know exactly what that meant or how to get there, but the desire wouldn't go away.

A friend of mine thought he had a good radio voice and should get into radio, but he was too nervous to apply at the station down the street from us. So I applied for him, just to show him how easy it was.

He never got the job. I did.

For four years, I worked in radio and became the number one ranked host in my market for my time slot. But even while I was succeeding in radio, I kept thinking about that original television calling. I started exploring the idea of starting a production company, even though I had no idea what that actually entailed.

Looking back, I can see how God was building my skill foundation, even when I didn't understand the bigger picture.

Radio taught me how to communicate clearly, how to connect with an audience, and how to not be afraid of expressing myself. Those skills became crucial later when I started creating content for my marketing agency and speaking face-to-face with business owners.

When I got fired from radio for being "over the top" and not conforming to rules I thought I knew better than, I switched career paths completely. I went from radio to being a sales manager at Borders Books and Music, then to journalism.

While working as a journalist, I earned a bachelor's degree in journalism and a master's degree in screenwriting. The journalism work taught me how to research, how to write clearly, and how to meet deadlines. The screenwriting degree taught me storytelling, which became essential for creating compelling marketing content.

During this time, I started noticing businesses that needed help with social media marketing. That's when the idea for a marketing agency began forming.

Your skills fall into three categories:

Natural Talents – Things you've always been good at, even before you received formal training. For me, communication and storytelling came naturally, even before I had any formal training.

Developed Skills – Abilities you've built through education, experience, or intentional practice. My degrees in journalism and screenwriting, my experience in radio and sales, all developed skills that seemed unrelated at the time but became the foundation of my business.

Excited-to-Learn Skills – Areas where you don't have expertise yet, but you're genuinely excited about developing it. When I started learning about content creation and social media marketing, I was excited to dive deeper, even though it was completely new territory.

The key insight is this: God doesn't waste anything. Every job, every experience, every skill you've developed has been preparing you for something. The business you're called to build will likely require a unique combination of everything you've learned so far.

Here's what I discovered when I stopped looking at individual skills and started looking at combinations: I wasn't just a writer, or just a former radio host, or just someone who understood marketing. I was someone who could combine storytelling, communication skills, and marketing knowledge to help businesses connect with their audiences in authentic ways.

That combination made me uniquely qualified to serve a specific group of people in a specific way.

Here's how to identify your skill foundation:

Make three lists. First, write down everything you're naturally good at. Don't overthink this. What do people consistently compliment you on? What feels easy to you that seems hard for others?

Second, list everything you've developed skills in through work, education, or experience. Include things that might not seem "business-relevant." Every experience has taught you something valuable.

Third, write down areas you're genuinely excited to learn more about. Not things you think you should be interested in, but things that actually capture your curiosity.

Look for patterns and intersections. Your unique business foundation is probably hiding in the overlap.

Question 2: SERVICE – Who do you feel called to serve?

This is where most business advice gets it backwards.

Most experts tell you to find a profitable market first, then figure out how to serve it. But that approach often leads to businesses that feel hollow, even when they're successful.

The faith-driven approach is different: start with who you feel called to serve, then figure out how to serve them profitably.

This doesn't mean you ignore market realities. It means you start with compassion and then apply business wisdom to turn that compassion into sustainable service. Nehemiah's story shows us exactly what this compassion-driven approach looks like in practice.

The Nehemiah Principle: Faithful Service Before Personal Gain

Nehemiah was a cupbearer to the Persian king—a comfortable, secure position in the royal court. But when he heard that Jerusalem's walls were broken down and his people were living in disgrace and vulnerability, he gave up his security to lead the massive project of rebuilding the city's defense. He wasn't thinking about starting a business or making money. He was moved by genuine compassion for their situation.

"And it came to pass, when I heard these words, that I sat down and wept, and mourned certain days, and fasted, and prayed before the God of heaven." (Nehemiah 1:4, KJV)

Nehemiah's response shows us the heart behind true calling—he felt burdened for specific people facing real problems. He didn't ask "What's the most profitable opportunity in Jerusalem?" He asked "How can I help my people who are suffering?"

This is the same principle that should drive your business decisions. When you start with genuine compassion for the people you want to serve, then figure out how to serve them sustainably and profitably, you're building on the right foundation.

Nehemiah organized resources, managed people, and completed a massive project—all skills that translate directly to entrepreneurship. His motivation wasn't monetary profit; but his faithful service established him as a trusted leader and governor. The walls he built protected generations of his people, and his legacy of faithful leadership opened doors for continued influence and impact.

Your business can have the same heart—serving others first—while also generating the income and influence you need to continue making a difference.

Who are you called to serve?

This question has layers. Start with compassion: whose problems keep you up at night? What group of people do you find yourself consistently concerned about?

Your calling to serve often shows up as a burden that won't go away. You see a problem that others seem to ignore, and you can't stop thinking about solutions.

But compassion alone isn't enough to build a sustainable business. You also need to consider:

Can you reach them? Do you have access to the people you want to serve? Can you find them, communicate with them, and build relationships with them?

Can they pay for solutions? This isn't about being greedy. It's about being realistic. If the people you want to serve don't have the resources to pay for help, you'll need to find a different business model or a different way to serve them.

Do you understand their world? The best businesses are built by people who deeply understand the problems they're solving. Either you've experienced the problem yourself, or you've spent enough time with people who have to truly understand what they're going through.

Sometimes the people you're called to serve aren't obvious at first. I initially thought I wanted to help any business that needed marketing. But as I started working with clients, I realized I was most effective with Christian business owners and faith-based organizations. They seemed to understand the importance of patience, the need to invest in order to see returns, and the value of building something with integrity.

Here's how to identify who you're called to serve:

Start with problems that make you angry or sad. What injustices bother you? What needs do you see that others seem to ignore?

Then get specific. Instead of "small business owners," think "family-owned restaurants struggling with online ordering systems." Instead of "people who need to lose weight," think "busy moms who want to get healthy but don't have time for complicated meal plans."

The more specific you get, the easier it becomes to understand their real problems and create solutions they'll actually pay for.

Question 3: SUSTAINABILITY – Can this model support your desired life?

This is the question most faith-driven entrepreneurs skip, and it's the reason so many of them burn out.

They get excited about serving people and solving problems, but they don't think through whether the business model can actually support the life God is calling them to live.

I learned this lesson the hard way when I first started my marketing agency.

My initial idea was to offer comprehensive social media management for small businesses at what I thought was an affordable price point. I figured if I could help more businesses by keeping my prices low, that was the right thing to do.

What I quickly discovered was that doing marketing right takes significant time and expertise. You can't effectively manage someone's entire social media presence, create quality content, engage with their audience, and track results for $200 a month. It's impossible.

I was working 60-hour weeks, barely making ends meet, and delivering subpar results because I didn't have enough time to do the work properly. That wasn't serving anyone well.

I had to make a hard decision: raise my prices significantly and focus on fewer clients, or burn out completely.

I chose to raise my prices and get selective about the clients I worked with. This meant turning away some potential customers, but it allowed me to deliver exceptional results for the clients I did take on. It also created a sustainable business model that didn't require me to work around the clock.

Sustainability isn't just about money, though money is part of it. It's about whether you can build this business in a way that enhances your life instead of consuming it.

The Financial Reality

Let's start with the money question, because ignoring it doesn't make it go away.

How much do you actually need to make for this business to work? Not how much you want to make, but how much you need to make.

Add up your basic living expenses. Include your mortgage or rent, utilities, food, transportation, insurance, and debt payments. Don't forget to include money for savings, giving, and some margin for unexpected expenses.

That's your baseline. Your business needs to generate enough profit to cover that number, plus taxes, plus business expenses.

Now, how long can you afford for the business to ramp up to that level? Do you have savings to cover your expenses for six months? A year? Or do you need the business to be profitable immediately?

Be honest about these numbers. Optimism is good, but financial pressure can kill a calling faster than almost anything else.

The Time Investment

How many hours per week can you realistically invest in this business? Not how many hours you think you should be able to work, but how many you can actually work given your current responsibilities.

Different business models require different time investments. A consulting business might require 20-30 hours per week once it's established, but 50-60 hours per week to get started. An online course business might require intense upfront work to create the content, then much less ongoing time to maintain.

Match your available time to business models that can work within those constraints.

The Stress Factor

Some businesses are inherently more stressful than others. Some require you to be "on" all the time. Others allow for more predictable schedules and clearer boundaries.

How much stress can you handle while still being the spouse, parent, and person God has called you to be? What's your tolerance for uncertainty, difficult customers, or financial ups and downs?

There's no right or wrong answer here. Some people thrive on high-stress, high-reward businesses. Others need more predictability and stability. The key is being honest about what works for your personality and your season of life.

The Family Factor

How will this business impact your most important relationships? Will it require travel that takes you away from your family? Will it require working hours that conflict with family time? Will it create financial stress that affects your marriage?

On the flip side, could this business enhance your family life? Could it provide more flexibility to be present for important moments? Could it create opportunities to involve your spouse or kids in meaningful ways?

Your business should serve your life, not consume it. If building this business requires you to sacrifice your most important relationships, it's not the right business for you, no matter how profitable it might be.

Question 4: SEASON – What season of life are you in right now?

This is the question that often gets overlooked, but it might be the most important one.

The business that would be perfect for you in ten years might be completely wrong for you right now. The business that's right for you now might not be the one you'll want to be running forever.

That's okay. God's calling on your life unfolds in seasons, and your business can too.

For me, starting with a marketing agency made sense for this season of my life. It allowed me to build skills, establish relationships, and generate revenue that I can eventually use to fund my film production company. The marketing agency is serving my current season while positioning me for the next one.

Available Capital vs. Bootstrap Mode

Do you have money to invest in getting started, or do you need to bootstrap everything?

If you have capital available, you can consider businesses that require upfront investment in inventory, equipment, or marketing. If you're bootstrapping, you need to focus on businesses that can start generating revenue quickly with minimal upfront costs.

Risk Tolerance Based on Responsibilities

Your risk tolerance changes based on your responsibilities. If you're single with no dependents, you can afford to take bigger risks than if you're supporting a family.

If you're the primary breadwinner, you might need to start your business as a side project while keeping your day job. If your spouse has a stable income, you might be able to focus on the business full-time from the beginning.

Energy and Health Considerations

Be honest about your current energy levels and health situation. Some businesses require physical stamina. Others are more mentally demanding. Some require you to be "on" and social most of the time. Others allow for more solitary, focused work.

Choose a business model that matches not just your skills and calling, but your current capacity.

Bringing It All Together

The Clarity Filter isn't about finding the perfect business. It's about finding the right business for you, in this season, with the skills and calling God has given you.

When you can answer all four questions clearly, you'll have a foundation for making a decision that you can build on with confidence.

My whiteboard looked very different after I worked through these questions. Instead of a long list of random business ideas, I could see how everything I'd experienced had been preparing me for this specific calling: helping established small businesses tell their stories and connect with their customers through authentic marketing.

More importantly, I had criteria for making decisions about pricing, client selection, and business model. I knew what I was looking for, and I knew why.

That clarity made all the difference.

In the next chapter, we'll address a crucial mindset shift you need to make before choosing any business model, then we'll explore the specific options available to you.

THE CLARITY FILTER—ACTION CHECKLIST

- SKILL Assessment

    - List everything you're naturally good at (ask friends/family if needed)

    - Write down all skills you've developed through work, education, or experience

    - Identify 3 areas you're genuinely excited to learn more about

    - Look for patterns and intersections between your lists

- SERVICE Identification

    - Write down problems that make you angry or sad

- Identify specific groups of people you feel drawn to help

  - Get specific: instead of "small business owners," write "family-owned restaurants struggling with online ordering"

- Research whether your target audience can afford solutions

- SUSTAINABILITY Evaluation

  - Calculate your actual monthly expenses (include savings and giving)

  - Determine how long you can afford for business to ramp up

  - Honestly assess how many hours per week you can invest

  - Consider your stress tolerance and family impact

- SEASON Assessment

  - Evaluate your current life stage and responsibilities

  - Determine your available capital vs. bootstrap needs

  - Assess your risk tolerance based on current situation

  - Consider your energy levels and health constraints

- Integration

  - Choose 2-3 business models that align with all four areas

  - Eliminate options that don't fit your current season

  - Rank remaining options by excitement and feasibility

4

THE BUSINESS MODELS MENU

11 types of businesses and what they really require

Your Job Is Not Your Identity

Here's something most people don't understand about choosing a business: the work you've been doing isn't necessarily the work you're called to do.

I worked as a radio-personality for about four years, spread across a six-year timeframe. I was good at it. I was ranked number one in my market for my time slot. But radio wasn't my identity. It was just preparation for what God was actually calling me to build.

The difference between me and some of my colleagues was simple: they believed their job was their identity. I believed my job was my training ground.

When I got fired from radio the second time for not conforming to corporate rules, some people thought I'd failed. But I knew God was redirecting me toward something bigger.

My former colleagues who stayed in radio? Some of them are still there, decades later. Some are happy, and if that's truly their calling, I respect that. But others are miserable, stuck in an identity that no longer serves them or the people they could be helping.

I've watched several former colleagues struggle when they lost their radio jobs. They became hermits, embarrassed that people might see them differently. Some even went backwards, trying to get back into radio instead of moving forward into what God had next for them.

Here's what I learned: when your job becomes your identity, you stop growing. You stop asking what God wants you to do next. You start worshipping your position instead of your purpose.

The Bible warns us not to look backward. Lot's wife looked back at Sodom and became a pillar of salt. The Israelites wanted to go back to Egypt when the wilderness got hard. Looking backward keeps you from moving into what God has prepared ahead.

The Corporate Trap

Things aren't the way they used to be. Most corporate jobs don't offer the security they once did. Pensions are rare. Benefits are shrinking. Loyalty goes one direction only.

Yet people still cling to jobs that drain their souls, thinking that staying in one place for thirty or forty years is somehow noble or safe.

I knew this back in the '90s when I was in high school. It didn't make sense to me then to stay in one place for decades, and it makes even less sense now. The gig economy exists because people finally figured out what I knew as a teenager: your security comes from your skills and your relationship with God, not from your employer's promises.

I watched colleagues in radio who made their job their god. They couldn't imagine doing anything else. They never developed skills beyond telling jokes on the air and promoting music shows. After thirty years, they had nothing to show for it except memories and regrets. Some of them died earlier than they should have. Maybe it was the lifestyle, maybe it was the stress, maybe it was just the slow death that comes from never living up to your potential.

I knew one guy who died in a car wreck on his way to his morning show. He'd spent years complaining on social media about his boss, his station, his situation. But he never left because he thought radio was who he was, not just what he did. He left virtually nothing behind except memories for the people who loved him. No meaningful impact. No fulfillment of the unique design God had given him.

Asking the Right Question

Here's the truth most people miss: you can come close to your Father in heaven by asking Him to come into your presence and you into His. Whatever you need, He has it. You just need to ask.

If you want to know what business you should be running, ask Him. You might not get a burning bush or a physical appearance of Jesus, but the signs will be made clear if you're genuinely seeking His guidance.

The question isn't "How can I turn my current job into a business?" The question is "What has God been preparing me to build through all my experiences?"

Sometimes the business you're called to start has nothing to do with your current job. Sometimes it uses skills you developed in your job but applies them in a completely different way. Sometimes it's the thing you've been thinking about on the side while you've been earning a paycheck doing something else.

The Menu Approach

Instead of trying to force your current job into a business model, let's look at what's actually available to you. Think of this as a menu of the most common and proven business model categories, each with its own requirements, challenges, and opportunities. While your specific business idea might be a unique variation or combination of these models, understanding these foundational types will help you evaluate any opportunity through the right lens.

But before we dive into specific models, you need to understand something crucial: not every business model will fit your unique combination of skills, calling, and season of life. That's why we worked through the Clarity Filter first.

As you read through these options, filter each one through those four questions:

1. Does this align with my skills or excited-to-learn areas?

2. Does this serve the people I feel called to help?

3. Can this model support my desired life sustainably?

4. Does this fit my current season?

Digital-First Business Models

Can be done online, from anywhere. Low startup cost. High time leverage.

1. Service-Based Business (Done-for-You)

What it looks like: You do specific work for clients. This could be writing, design, marketing, bookkeeping, virtual assistance, or any other skill-based service.

What people don't tell you: You're trading time for money, which limits your income potential unless you raise rates significantly or build a team. Client management can be demanding, and you're only as secure as your next contract.

How it aligns with Christian stewardship: You're using your God-given talents to serve others directly. You can choose clients whose values align with yours and build relationships that go beyond just business transactions.

Realistic expectations: $50,000-$150,000 annually as a solo practitioner, potentially much more with a team. Expect 6-12 months to build a steady client base.

Time investment: 40-60 hours per week initially, potentially 30-40 once established.

2. Coaching & Courses

What it looks like: Teaching what you know through one-on-one coaching, group programs, or online courses. This could be business coaching, life coaching, skill development, or any area where you have expertise.

What people don't tell you: Creating quality educational content takes significant time upfront. You need to be comfortable being visible and marketing yourself. Not everyone is cut out to be a teacher, even if they have expertise.

How it aligns with Christian stewardship: You're multiplying your impact by teaching others. You can integrate biblical principles into your teaching and help people grow in areas that matter.

Realistic expectations: Highly variable. Successful coaches can make $100,000-$500,000+ annually, but many struggle to reach $50,000. Courses can generate passive income, but only after significant upfront investment.

Time investment: 50-70 hours per week initially to create content and build audience, 20-40 hours once established.

3. Content Creation / Personal Brand

What it looks like: Building an audience through YouTube, Instagram, blogging, podcasting, or other platforms, then monetizing through sponsorships, affiliate marketing, or your own products.

What people don't tell you: Building a significant audience takes years, not months. You need to be comfortable being public about your life and opinions. Income is unpredictable and platform-dependent.

How it aligns with Christian stewardship: You can use your platform to share your faith and values while serving your audience. Your content can encourage, educate, and inspire others.

Realistic expectations: Most content creators make very little. Those who succeed can make $50,000-$1,000,000+ annually, but it typically takes 2-5 years to reach significant income levels.

Time investment: 40-60 hours per week consistently. Content creation is time-intensive and never stops.

4. Digital Products

What it looks like: Creating and selling templates, printables, guides, eBooks, software tools, or apps that solve specific problems for your target market.

What people don't tell you: Creating quality digital products takes longer than expected. Marketing is crucial and ongoing. You need systems for delivery, customer service, and updates.

How it aligns with Christian stewardship: You can create resources that genuinely help people solve problems or improve their lives. Once created, products can serve many people without additional time investment from you.

Realistic expectations: $10,000-$100,000+ annually possible, but most digital product creators make less than $25,000. Success depends heavily on marketing and finding the right market fit.

Time investment: 30-50 hours per week initially to create and launch products, 10-20 hours per week for ongoing marketing and customer service.

5. Affiliate Marketing

What it looks like: Promoting other people's products or services and earning commissions on sales. This often combines with content creation or email marketing.

What people don't tell you: Building trust with your audience takes time, and you need significant traffic to generate meaningful income. You're dependent on other companies' products and commission structures.

How it aligns with Christian stewardship: You can promote products you genuinely believe in and that serve your audience well. Focus on being honest about what you recommend and why.

Realistic expectations: $500-$50,000+ annually, with most affiliate marketers making less than $10,000. Success requires significant audience building and strategic promotion.

Time investment: 20-40 hours per week, mostly focused on content creation and audience building.

6. Software/Apps

What it looks like: Creating digital tools that solve specific problems for businesses or consumers. This could be mobile apps, web applications, or software-as-a-service products.

What people don't tell you: Development costs are high, either in time if you learn to code or money if you hire developers. Most apps fail. Ongoing maintenance and updates are required.

How it aligns with Christian stewardship: You can create tools that genuinely make people's lives easier or more productive. Technology can be a powerful way to serve others at scale.

Realistic expectations: Highly variable. Successful apps can generate $100,000-$10,000,000+ annually, but most make very little. Expect 2-5 years before significant revenue.

Time investment: 60-80 hours per week initially if you're learning to develop, 40-60 hours if you're managing developers and handling business aspects.

Operational / Local Service Businesses

Location-based, often labor-intensive. Higher startup costs. Scalable with systems.

7. Local Services

What it looks like: Providing services in your local area such as cleaning, landscaping, home maintenance, pet services, or other location-dependent work.

What people don't tell you: You're limited by geography and local market size. Physical work can be demanding. Weather, seasonality, and local economic conditions affect your business.

How it aligns with Christian stewardship: You're serving your immediate community and can build personal relationships with clients. You can be a positive presence in your neighborhood.

Realistic expectations: $40,000-$150,000+ annually, depending on the service and market. Higher-end services like specialized home improvement can generate more.

Time investment: 40-60 hours per week, including travel time between jobs.

8. Licensed Professions

What it looks like: Businesses that require professional licenses such as real estate, insurance, financial planning, healthcare services, or legal services.

What people don't tell you: Licensing requirements can be extensive and expensive. Regulations are strict. Continuing education is usually required. Some professions have high liability.

How it aligns with Christian stewardship: You can serve people during important life transitions and decisions. Your integrity and values can set you apart in fields that sometimes have trust issues.

Realistic expectations: $50,000-$500,000+ annually, depending on the profession and market. Real estate and financial services can be particularly lucrative.

Time investment: 40-60 hours per week, with some professions requiring evening and weekend availability.

9. Product-Based Business

What it looks like: Creating, manufacturing, or reselling physical products. This could include food products, crafts, retail items, or e-commerce.

What people don't tell you: Inventory management is complex and expensive. Shipping, returns, and customer service require systems. Margins can be thin, especially when starting out.

How it aligns with Christian stewardship: You can create products that genuinely improve people's lives. Physical products can be a tangible way to serve others' needs.

Realistic expectations: $30,000-$200,000+ annually, but many product businesses struggle with profitability. Success depends heavily on finding the right product-market fit.

Time investment: 50-70 hours per week, including production, marketing, and fulfillment.

10. Trades & Construction

What it looks like: Skilled labor businesses such as plumbing, electrical work, HVAC, carpentry, or general contracting. Can also include house flipping or remodeling.

What people don't tell you: Physical demands are high. Licensing and insurance requirements vary by location. Economic downturns significantly impact construction-related businesses.

How it aligns with Christian stewardship: You're using your hands to create and fix things, which reflects God's creative nature. You can serve families by improving their homes and living conditions.

Realistic expectations: $50,000-$200,000+ annually for skilled trades. House flipping can generate higher returns but with much higher risk.

Time investment: 40-60 hours per week, with potential for seasonal variations.

11. Investment & Business Acquisition

What it looks like: Buying existing businesses to improve and resell, investing in startups or established companies, or building a portfolio of income-generating assets. This could include business flipping, becoming a silent partner in multiple ventures, or creating an investment fund.

What people don't tell you: Requires significant capital or knowledge of creative financing. Due diligence is time-intensive and requires understanding of financial statements, market conditions, and business operations. Returns can be substantial but are never guaranteed.

How it aligns with Christian stewardship: You're helping existing businesses reach their potential and creating jobs. You can choose to invest only in businesses that align with your values and contribute positively to their communities.

Realistic expectations: Highly variable based on capital available and market knowledge. Could range from $50,000-$1,000,000+ annually, but requires substantial upfront investment or financing knowledge.

Time investment: 20-40 hours per week for active investors, less for passive investors with good systems.

Filtering Through Your Calling

As you read through these options, some probably resonated more than others. That's your first clue about where to focus your attention.

But don't choose based on income potential alone. Choose based on alignment with your unique design and calling.

For me, the service-based marketing business aligned perfectly with my combination of communication skills, writing ability, and desire to help established businesses tell their stories better. It fit my current season, allowed me to serve people I cared about, and created a sustainable income while building toward my longer-term vision of film production.

Your path will be different because your calling is different.

When you're facing business decisions and don't know which direction to go, don't rely solely on market research or expert advice. James 1:5 gives us a better starting point: "If any of you lack wisdom, let him ask of God, that giveth to all men liberally, and upbraideth not; and it shall be given him." God promises to give wisdom generously to those who ask for it. Before you analyze spreadsheets or poll your advisors, ask the One who sees the whole picture and wants your business to succeed for the right reasons.

In the next chapter, we'll talk about how to test your chosen business model before you fully commit to it. Because even with analysis and prayer, you won't know for sure until you try.

But first, you need to choose. Not the perfect business, but the right business for you, right now, in this season, with the skills and calling God has given you.

Which one is calling to you?

5

THE REALITY CHECK

Get brutally honest before you decide

I was staring at my bank statement on a Tuesday morning in 2019, and something hit me that I'd never considered before.

The take-home pay from my journalism job was $1,847 that month. After rent, utilities, groceries, and gas, I had maybe $200 left over. I was 43 years old, had two college degrees, and was barely scraping by.

But instead of feeling defeated, I felt something unexpected: relief.

Because I finally understood what God had been doing all those years.

He'd been keeping my wages low on purpose. Not to punish me, but to prepare me.

The Gift of Low Wages

Looking back, I can see the pattern clearly now. From 1999 to 2004, I made $18,000 a year as a radio personality (often called a disc jockey). I was ranked number one in the market for my time slot, working my tail off to make my show entertaining and topical, doing my own research and production. But I was making poverty wages.

From 2006 to 2010, I earned $32,000 a year as a sales manager at Borders Books and Music. In 2013, I landed my first full-time job in journalism and made $30,000 a year. And when I left journalism and took a job as a legal assistant, I earned $18 an hour.

For more than a decade, my take-home pay was often less than $2,000 a month.

At the time, I was scared about money. I shouldn't have been, because God tells us not to worry, that He'll provide everything we need. Looking back, He did exactly that. But I was focused on the fear instead of the preparation.

Here's what I realize now: if I'd been making $80,000 a year in radio, it would have been much harder to accept getting fired and moving on to the next thing. If I'd been comfortable in any of those jobs, I might have stayed stuck in someone else's vision for my life instead of discovering what God was calling me to build.

The low wages weren't punishment. They were motivation.

When you're making less than $2,000 a month, it's not hard to imagine self-employment opportunities that can easily replace that amount. The bar isn't set impossibly high. You don't need to build a million-dollar business to improve your situation. You just need to build something sustainable that serves people well.

The Stability Myth

Here's something most people don't understand: owning your own business is actually the most stable way to make a living. Everything else is just as unpredictable.

I got fired from radio twice. I got laid off from Borders when the company went bankrupt. Newspapers have been cutting staff for years. Every job I've ever had has been just as volatile as running my own business.

The difference is this: when you work for someone else, you have no control over the volatility. When you work for yourself, you can at least influence the outcome.

If I lose a client today, I have the power to go get another one. I can adjust my pricing, change my services, or pivot my approach. When I worked for newspapers, if they decided to eliminate my position, I had no recourse except to start job hunting in an industry that was shrinking.

There are no guarantees in business, but there were no guarantees working for someone else either. At least now I get to bet on myself instead of betting on someone else's vision for their company.

The Hard Truths

Before you choose what business to start, you need to get brutally honest about five key areas. These aren't the fun, inspiring questions. These are the practical realities that will determine whether your business actually works.

Most faith-driven entrepreneurs skip this step because it feels unspiritual to focus on money and logistics. But stewardship requires wisdom, and wisdom means being realistic about what you're getting into.

The Money Talk: What do you actually need to make this work?

Let's start with the question everyone wants to avoid: how much money do you actually need to make for this business to work?

Not how much you want to make. Not how much you think you deserve to make. How much you need to make to cover your responsibilities and live the life God is calling you to live.

Start by calculating your monthly survival number. What does it actually cost you to live? Include the non-negotiables: housing, utilities, food, transportation, insurance, and any debt payments you're committed to. Then add in the things that matter to your values: money for savings, giving, and a small buffer for life's surprises.

That's your baseline. Your business needs to generate enough profit to cover that number, plus business expenses and taxes.

Next, be realistic about your runway. How many months can you cover your expenses while the business grows? If you have a year's worth of savings, you can afford to build more slowly. If you need income next month, you need a business model that can generate revenue quickly.

Be honest about these numbers. Optimism is good, but financial pressure can kill a calling faster than almost anything else.

Here's what I discovered: when your baseline is reasonable, almost any business model becomes viable. When I was making $30,000 as a journalist, I knew that if I could generate $3,000 a month in marketing services, I'd already be ahead. That made the decision to start my agency much easier.

If you're currently making $100,000 a year, you need a business model that can realistically reach that level within a reasonable timeframe. If you're making $35,000, you have more flexibility to start small and grow gradually.

The key is being realistic about both your needs and the timeline for your chosen business model to meet those needs.

The Time Truth: How many hours can you realistically invest?

Here's where most people lie to themselves. They think about how many hours they wish they could work on their business, not how many hours they can actually work given their current responsibilities.

If you're married with young kids, your available time looks different than if you're single or if your kids are grown. If you're currently working a full-time job, you're probably looking at evenings and weekends to start.

Different business models require different time investments. A consulting business might require 20-30 hours per week once it's established, but 50-60 hours per week to get started. An online course business might require intense upfront work to create the content, then much less ongoing time to maintain.

Match your available time to business models that can work within those constraints.

After I got laid off from Borders Books and Music and decided to become a journalist and earn a master's degree in screenwriting, I dedicated every hour outside of my nine-to-five job to building toward my business. That meant sacrifices. My dedication to stacking skills and figuring out my blueprint came at a cost. I lost touch with some close friends and even family.

I'm not saying the choice I made is right for everyone. I'm saying you need to be honest about what your business will require and what you're willing to give up to build it.

During those years, I closed my skill gap. I learned content creation, marketing strategy, client management, and storytelling. I worked at different companies and observed what other people were doing well and poorly. All of that preparation positioned me to answer the competition question when I finally launched my agency.

But it came at a cost. Make sure you're clear about what you're willing to pay before you start.

The Family Factor: How will this impact your most important relationships?

Your business should serve your life, not consume it. If building this business requires you to sacrifice your most important relationships, it's not the right business for you, no matter how profitable it might be.

Will this business require travel that takes you away from your family? Will it require working hours that conflict with family time? Will it create financial stress that affects your marriage?

On the flip side, could this business enhance your family life? Could it provide more flexibility to be present for important moments? Could it create opportunities to involve your spouse or kids in meaningful ways?

I chose to prioritize building my business over building a family during my preparation years. That was the right choice for my situation and calling, but it might be completely wrong for yours.

If you're married, this decision affects more than just you. Your spouse needs to be on board with the time investment, the financial risk, and the lifestyle changes that come with entrepreneurship. If you have kids, you need to consider how your business building will impact your availability for their activities and needs.

There's no right or wrong answer here. There's only what's right for your family in your current season.

The Skill Gap: What do you need to learn and how long will it take?

Every business requires skills you don't currently have. The question is whether you're willing to develop those skills and how long it will take.

Some skills can be learned quickly through online courses or books. Others require years of practice to develop competency. Some require formal education or certification.

Be realistic about your learning curve. If you're naturally good with people but have never done sales, you can probably learn basic sales skills relatively quickly. If you're great at your craft but have never run a business, you'll need to learn marketing, accounting, client management, and operations.

I had an advantage when I started my marketing agency because I'd been developing the core skills for years without realizing it. My journalism background taught me research and writing. My radio experience taught me communication and audience awareness. My screenwriting education taught me storytelling.

But I still had to learn client management, pricing strategy, project management, and business operations. Those skills took time to develop, and I made plenty of mistakes along the way.

Make a list of the skills your chosen business model requires. Be honest about which ones you have, which ones you can learn quickly, and which ones will take significant time to develop. Factor that learning time into your timeline and expectations.

The Competition Question: Why will people choose you?

This is the question that separates successful businesses from failed ones. It's not enough to be good at what you do. You need to be able to articulate why someone should choose you over all the other options available to them.

What makes you different? What unique combination of skills, experience, and perspective do you bring to the market?

For me, the answer became clear after years of working in different industries and observing how other marketers operated. I could speak to business owners' pain points because I'd worked in businesses. I could tell their stories better than most content creators because I'm a trained storyteller. I could write copy that sounded human instead of robotic because I understand how to connect with an audience.

When I sell my marketing services, I lead with the fact that I'm a copywriter and screenwriter, that I'm a storyteller who doesn't write like a robot. I can speak to target audiences' pain points and persuade with words because I understand both the technical and emotional sides of communication.

That combination of skills and experience is what sets me apart from the 22-year-old college graduate who knows the basics of social media marketing but has never run a business or written copy that actually converts.

Your competitive advantage might be your industry experience, your unique skill combination, your personal story, or your approach to serving clients. But you need to be able to articulate it clearly, both to yourself and to potential customers.

Bringing It All Together

These five questions aren't meant to discourage you from starting a business. They're meant to help you choose the right business and approach it with realistic expectations.

When I worked through these questions honestly, I realized that a marketing agency was the perfect fit for my current situation. The financial requirements were manageable based on my low baseline expenses. The time investment worked with my single status and willingness to work evenings and weekends. The skill gap was minimal because of all my preparation. And I had a clear competitive advantage based on my unique background.

Plus, it positioned me to eventually build the film production company I'd been dreaming about for years. The marketing agency isn't my final destination. It's the vehicle that will get me there.

Your answers to these questions will help you choose not just any business, but the right business for your unique situation and calling.

Don't skip this step. The time you spend being realistic about these factors will save you years of building something that doesn't actually work for your life.

THE REALITY CHECK—ACTION CHECKLIST

- Financial Reality Check

    - Calculate your survival number (monthly expenses + taxes + business costs)

- ○ Determine your available runway (savings ÷ monthly expenses)

- ○ Set realistic timeline for profitability based on chosen business model

- ○ Identify potential funding sources if needed

- Time Investment Assessment

  - ○ Map out your current weekly schedule

  - ○ Identify available hours for business building

  - ○ Compare time requirements of different business models

  - ○ Plan how to protect family/rest time

- Skill Gap Analysis

  - ○ List skills required for your chosen business model

  - ○ Identify which skills you have vs. need to develop

  - ○ Estimate learning time for each missing skill

  - ○ Create learning plan with realistic timelines

- Competition Research

  - ○ Identify 5-10 competitors in your market

  - ○ Analyze their pricing, services, and positioning

  - ○ Determine your unique competitive advantage

  - ○ Write your "why choose me" statement

- Family Alignment

- Discuss business plans with spouse/family

- Address concerns about time, money, and risk

- Get commitment for support during startup phase

- Set boundaries and expectations for family time

6

SPIRITUAL DUE DILIGENCE

Don't just choose, discern

Here's something most business books won't tell you: there's literal power in prayer. Not just comfort or peace of mind, but actual, tangible power that can transform your business and your life.

I didn't always understand this. Growing up, my parents were faithful people. We prayed before meals and went to church regularly when I was young. But as an adult, my prayer life became sporadic. I'd pray before eating, and occasionally in the shower, but it wasn't a consistent part of my life.

When I did pray about my future, I kept it simple. I asked God for three things: good health, knowledge and wisdom, and the confidence that I could figure everything else out from there. I never prayed for money directly. While other people were asking God to help them pay bills or provide for their families, I figured if I had health and wisdom, I could handle the financial part myself.

And for years, that approach worked. God gave me exactly what I asked for. I maintained good health, gained knowledge through my various jobs and education, and developed wisdom through experience. I was figuring things out, just like I'd asked.

But when I finally went out on my own and money got tight, when I didn't know if I was going to land another client that was a good fit, something shifted. For the first time in my adult life, I started praying specifically for business success and financial provision.

That's when things started happening.

Not immediately, and not in the way I expected. I didn't get a sudden influx of clients or a windfall of cash. Instead, I started getting ideas. Solutions to problems I didn't even know I had. Insights into skills I didn't realize I was missing.

God wasn't just giving me money. He was showing me what I needed to learn to earn the money He wanted to bless me with.

I'd discover gaps in my knowledge about client management, or realize I needed to understand a particular marketing strategy better, or see that I was pricing my services incorrectly. Each revelation led to action, and each action led to better results.

The money came, but it came through growth, not through shortcuts.

Pray Then Plan: Partnering with God in the Process

Most entrepreneurs approach business planning like this: they come up with an idea, create a plan, work the plan, and then pray that God blesses their efforts.

But what if we flipped that approach?

What if instead of asking God to bless our predetermined plans, we started by asking Him what He wants us to build?

This doesn't mean sitting around waiting for a burning bush or an audible voice from heaven. Most of the time, God's guidance comes through ideas, opportunities, open doors, and closed doors. It comes through the people He brings into your life and the problems He places on your heart.

But you have to be listening for it.

When I finally started praying specifically about my business, asking God to show me what I was missing and where He wanted me to go next, the answers started coming. Not all at once, and not always in ways I expected, but consistently enough that I couldn't ignore the pattern.

Sometimes the answer was a new skill I needed to develop. Sometimes it was a client I needed to let go of because they weren't aligned with where God was taking me. Sometimes it was a pricing change or a service adjustment that seemed risky but felt right.

The key was learning to recognize His voice in the midst of all the other voices competing for my attention. The voice of fear that told me to play it safe. The voice of greed that told me to take every opportunity. The voice of comparison that told me to copy what others were doing.

God's voice was different. It was the voice that led me toward growth, toward serving others better, toward building something that aligned with His purposes for my life.

This process of learning to recognize and follow God's guidance in business decisions is exactly what Scripture calls us to do. Proverbs 16:3 teaches us: "Commit thy works unto the Lord, and thy thoughts shall be established." Notice the order—first you commit your work to God, then your thoughts and plans become clear and established. Most entrepreneurs do this backwards. They establish their thoughts first, then ask God to bless their work.

90 Days to Data: Testing Before You Commit

Faith doesn't mean being foolish. God gave you a brain, and He expects you to use it. That's why spiritual discernment should be paired with practical testing.

Before you quit your job, invest your life savings, or make any major commitment to a business idea, test it on a smaller scale first.

Give yourself 90 days to gather real data about your business idea. Not theoretical data or wishful thinking, but actual results from real attempts to serve real customers.

If you're thinking about starting a consulting business, offer to help three people for free in exchange for honest feedback and testimonials. If you're considering an online course, create a mini-version and see if people will actually buy it. If you want to start a service-based business, take on a few small projects to understand what the work actually involves.

This 90-day testing period serves two purposes. First, it gives you practical information about whether your business idea actually works in the real world. Second, it gives God time to confirm or redirect your plans through the results you see.

During my testing phase with the marketing agency, I learned that my initial pricing was too low, that certain types of clients were a poor fit for my services, and that I needed to develop better systems for managing projects. I also discovered that I genuinely enjoyed the work and that clients were getting real results from my efforts.

Those 90 days of testing saved me from making costly mistakes and gave me confidence to move forward with a refined version of my original plan.

Follow the complete testing process outlined in Appendix B: 90-Day Business Model Test Plan; and use Appendix D: 90-Day Decision Matrix to objectively evaluate your test results and make your go/no-go decision.

Peace or Pushback: Listening for Spiritual Confirmation

One of the most reliable ways to discern God's will for your business is to pay attention to the peace or pushback you feel as you move forward.

When you're moving in the right direction, there's usually a sense of peace that accompanies the work, even when it's challenging. You feel energized by the problems you're solving. You're excited about the people you're serving. The work feels meaningful, not just profitable.

When you're moving in the wrong direction, there's usually pushback. Not just external obstacles, but internal resistance. The work feels forced. You're constantly fighting against circumstances instead of flowing with them. You feel drained instead of energized.

This doesn't mean the right path will be easy. Building any business requires hard work, sacrifice, and perseverance. But there's a difference between the difficulty that comes from growth and the difficulty that comes from fighting against your calling.

I experienced this difference clearly when I was trying to decide between different business models. When I considered options that were purely profit-driven but didn't align with my skills or calling, everything felt like an uphill battle. When I focused on the marketing agency that combined my writing skills with my desire to help businesses tell their stories better, the pieces started falling into place.

The work was still hard, but it was the right kind of hard. It was challenging in ways that made me grow instead of ways that made me question whether I was on the right path.

Boaz Moments: Recognizing and Acting on God's Open Doors

Sometimes God's guidance comes through opportunities to do the right thing, even when it's inconvenient, challenging, and easier to walk away. These are what I call "Boaz moments," after the biblical story of Ruth and Boaz.

When Boaz learned he had the legal right to redeem Naomi's family line and marry Ruth, he didn't have to act on it. The responsibility and cost were substantial. It would require significant financial investment and personal commitment. He could have found reasons to decline or pass the responsibility to someone else.

Instead, Boaz chose to step up. He handled the legal proceedings properly, married Ruth, and secured her future. His decision to act on his opportunity to redeem created a legacy that extended far beyond what he could have imagined—their lineage led directly to King David and ultimately to Jesus.

The same principle applies in business. God opens doors and creates opportunities for you to serve others well, but you still have to choose whether to walk through them, especially when it's inconvenient or requires you to stretch beyond your comfort zone.

I had a Boaz moment that taught me this lesson clearly. I met with a potential client who owned a medical practice, and I pitched him digital marketing services that I knew would work—services I could prove results with and that would clearly benefit his business.

But when we sat down to discuss details, he didn't want those services. Instead, he wanted me to help him create video content for his political podcast and figure out how to monetize his social media channels. This wasn't what I wanted to do. I couldn't easily prove results, and if his podcast wasn't good, there wasn't much I could do to help him make money from it.

But I was willing to try, so I took the project and significantly undercharged him that first month. Once I got started, I realized the work was far more time-consuming than I'd anticipated. Matching visuals to podcast audio, creating engaging social media content, and trying to build an audience for something I had no control over—it was exhausting.

At the end of the month, I'd accomplished far less than I felt I should have, even though I'd undercharged him. I was discouraged and convinced he'd be upset about both the results and the cost. So I sent him an email explaining that I couldn't deliver what he wanted for the price I was charging—it was just too much work.

That's when he surprised me by offering to pay double what I'd originally quoted him.

I had a choice. I could have walked away from a difficult, tech-challenged client who wanted services outside my comfort zone. Or I could step up and figure out how to serve him well.

I chose to step up. It took months of learning new systems, teaching him technology he didn't understand, and developing strategies for monetizing content without having products to sell. There were times I thought he'd fire me because progress was slow and required so much input from him.

But we figured it out. He now has monetized social media channels that are generating income and offsetting what he pays me. We're building toward full profitability, and he's getting more views and listeners than ever before. He's been with me for over a year now, and we're discussing expanding into other areas of his business.

That Boaz moment—choosing to serve well when it would have been easier to walk away—turned into one of my most valuable client relationships. Sometimes the doors God opens require us to develop new skills and push beyond our comfort zones, but that's often where the greatest growth and opportunity lie.

Wise Counsel: Getting Input from Mature Believers Who Know Business

"Where no counsel is, the people fall: but in the multitude of counsellors there is safety." (Proverbs 11:14, KJV)

God rarely calls us to build businesses in isolation. He provides wise counselors to help us see blind spots, avoid mistakes, and make better decisions.

But not all counsel is created equal. You need input from people who understand both faith and business, who can help you discern God's will while also giving you practical advice about what actually works in the marketplace.

Look for mentors who have successfully built businesses while maintaining their integrity and their relationship with God. Find people who can pray with you about your decisions and also help you think through the practical implications of your choices.

Avoid counselors who tell you that faith and business don't mix, or that wanting to be profitable somehow compromises your spiritual life. Also avoid counselors who understand business but have no spiritual discernment to offer.

The best counselors are those who can help you see how God might be working through market opportunities, business relationships, and even setbacks to accomplish His purposes in your life.

I've been blessed with several mentors who helped me navigate key decisions in my business journey. They helped me see opportunities I was missing, warned me about potential pitfalls, and encouraged me to take steps of faith that I might have been too cautious to take on my own.

Their counsel didn't replace my need to seek God's guidance directly, but it provided confirmation and clarity that helped me move forward with confidence.

Open and Closed Doors: Reading the Signs God Gives You

God speaks through circumstances as much as He speaks through prayer and Scripture. Learning to read the signs He gives you through open and closed doors is crucial for business success.

Open doors might look like:

- Unexpected opportunities that align with your calling

- People who offer to help or collaborate without you asking

- Resources becoming available just when you need them

- Clients who find you instead of you having to chase them

- Skills or knowledge that come together in ways you didn't plan

Closed doors might look like:

- Repeated obstacles that prevent you from moving in a particular direction

- Lack of peace about a decision even when it looks good on paper

- Relationships or opportunities that consistently fall through

- Financial provision that doesn't come despite your best efforts

- Skills or resources that remain out of reach despite persistent effort

The key is learning to distinguish between doors that are closed by God and doors that are simply challenging to open. Sometimes God wants you to persevere through difficulty. Other times He wants you to recognize that He's redirecting you toward something better.

This discernment comes through prayer, wise counsel, and experience. The more you practice listening for God's guidance in your business decisions, the better you become at recognizing His voice.

Moving Forward with Confidence

Spiritual due diligence isn't about eliminating all risk or uncertainty from your business decisions. It's about making sure you're building something that aligns with God's purposes for your life and serves others in meaningful ways.

When you combine prayer with practical testing, when you seek wise counsel and pay attention to open and closed doors, when you listen for peace or pushback as you move forward, you can make business decisions with confidence.

Not because you have all the answers, but because you know you're not making the decisions alone.

In the next chapter, we'll talk about how to actually start building once you've discerned what God is calling you to create. We'll cover the practical steps for moving from idea to implementation while maintaining the spiritual foundation you've established.

But first, take time to work through this spiritual due diligence process for yourself. Don't rush into business building without first making sure you're building the right thing for the right reasons.

Your business is too important to build without God's guidance. And His guidance is too valuable to ignore in favor of your own understanding.

SPIRITUAL DUE DILIGENCE—ACTION CHECKLIST

- Prayer and Planning

  - Commit to daily prayer about your business direction

  - Ask God to reveal His will for your business calling

  - Pray for wisdom in decision-making (James 1:5)

  - Listen for His guidance through circumstances and peace

- 90-Day Testing Plan

  - Choose one business idea to test for 90 days

  - Define specific metrics to measure during testing

  - Offer services to 3 people (free or discounted) for feedback

  - Document what you learn about the business model

- Spiritual Confirmation

  - Pay attention to peace vs. pushback as you move forward

  - Notice open doors and closed doors

  - Journal about what you're sensing spiritually

  - Look for confirmation through multiple sources

- Wise Counsel

  - Identify 2-3 mature believers who understand business

  - Schedule conversations to get their input

  - Ask specific questions about your business direction

  - Consider their advice alongside your prayer time

- Scripture Study

  - Study biblical examples of entrepreneurs (Proverbs 31 woman, Lydia, etc.)

  - Meditate on Proverbs 16:3 regarding committing your work to the Lord

  - Read passages about stewardship and using your gifts

  - Apply biblical principles to your business planning

7

THE FAITHFUL STARTER STRATEGY

How to move in faith, not fear

I remember the exact moment I realized I was sabotaging my own success. I'd just been laid off from my full-time job as a legal assistant. My employer gave me two weeks' notice—they were changing their business model and no longer needed my position.

I had a choice: find another full-time job or go all-in on the marketing agency I'd been building on the side.

I chose the agency. I had the skills—a bachelor's in journalism, a master's in screenwriting, experience in content creation, SEO, ad writing, social media management, Google Ads, Facebook Ads. I could offer dozens of different services because I knew how to do them all.

But instead of immediately focusing on landing clients, I got stuck in preparation mode.

I spent weeks rebuilding my website. I created new lead magnets. I designed email sequences and sales funnels. I was trying to show an online presence that proved I was a legitimate marketer, which I already was.

Meanwhile, I was still paying contractors I'd been outsourcing work to when I had a full-time job. I should have stopped those payments immediately, but I thought I'd quickly land new clients to cover the costs.

Sixty days went by. Then ninety. I brought on one low-ticket client, but it wasn't nearly enough. I had to borrow money to keep things going.

The problem wasn't that I lacked skills or experience. The problem was that I was trying to be everything to everyone. Instead of saying "This is what I'm called to help people with," I was saying "What do you need? I can probably do that."

I was hiding behind perfectionism and calling it preparation. I had everything I needed to serve clients well, but I was too busy building systems to actually serve anyone.

That's when it hit me: I wasn't preparing anymore. I was procrastinating.

The Preparation Trap

Here's something nobody tells you about starting a business: you can prepare yourself right out of ever actually starting.

There's always one more course to take, one more system to build, one more piece of the puzzle to put in place before you're "ready." The problem is, you're never really ready. You just get to a point where you're ready enough.

Faith-driven entrepreneurs are especially susceptible to this trap because we want to honor God by doing things excellently. We think that means having everything perfect before we begin. But sometimes the most honoring thing we can do is start with what we have and trust God to fill in the gaps as we go.

This doesn't mean being reckless or unprepared. It means being prepared enough to serve people well, then learning and improving as you grow.

The difference between preparation and procrastination is simple: preparation moves you toward serving others, procrastination moves you toward serving your own need for certainty.

The enemy's greatest strategy isn't to make you fail—it's to keep you stuck in inaction. Jesus gave us the Great Commission in Matthew 28:19: "Go ye therefore, and teach all nations, baptizing them in the name of the Father, and of the Son, and of the Holy Ghost." Notice that it starts with "Go." Not "sit and wait," not "prepare until you're perfect," but "Go."

Satan knows that if he can keep you paralyzed by fear, perfectionism, or endless preparation, you'll never fulfill the calling God has placed on your life. Your business isn't just about making money—it's about going into your marketplace and demonstrating God's principles through how you serve others. But you can't do that if you never start.

Every day you delay taking action is another day the people you're called to serve continue struggling with problems you could solve. The enemy wants you stuck in planning mode forever because he knows that once you start moving, God will bless your faithful steps.

Don't Just Pray, Build: Combining Action with Faith

Remember Jacob's story? After working fourteen years to marry Rachel, he found himself with a family but still no wealth of his own. To change that, he made a deal with Laban to keep any future animals born with patterned markings as his wages.

Laban quickly agreed, but then immediately tried to rig the deal. That same day, he secretly removed all the speckled and spotted animals and put them under his sons' care, placing a three-day journey between them and Jacob. By doing so, Laban cut off Jacob's ability to breed those animals, making success look nearly impossible.

But Jacob didn't retaliate or complain. Nor did he just pray for favor and wait for God to drop blessings out of the sky. He partnered with God through action, wisdom, and relentless faith.

Jacob studied the flocks. He noticed patterns. He developed breeding strategies that seemed strange to others but made sense to him. He worked with quiet confidence, and God caused his herds to multiply.

"And the man increased exceedingly, and had much cattle, and maidservants, and menservants, and camels, and asses." (Genesis 30:43, KJV)

Jacob combined obedience to what he believed, ingenuity in what he observed, and faith in God's favor to produce a breakthrough strategy that built his wealth.

That pattern still works today.

Faith isn't passive. It's strategic obedience. It means showing up with your brain, your creativity, and your belief that God will bless the work of your hands, especially when you refuse to play dirty, even when others do.

Sometimes we say we're "waiting on God" when what we're really doing is waiting for certainty. But God rarely gives us certainty before He gives us opportunity. He gives us enough light for the next step, not the whole staircase.

Jacob didn't know his breeding strategies would work when he started implementing them. He just knew he had to do something, and he trusted God to honor his faithful efforts.

The same principle applies to your business. You don't need to see the whole path before you take the first step. You just need to take the first step with faith that God will guide the rest.

Creating Your Service Framework

Before you can effectively serve clients, you need to know exactly how you're going to get them from where they are to where they want to be. This isn't just about having skills—it's about having a systematic approach that you can repeat, refine, and communicate clearly to prospects.

Most new entrepreneurs skip this step and wonder why their sales conversations feel scattered or why clients seem confused about what they're actually buying.

The solution is creating a framework—a clear, step-by-step process that guides how you deliver results.

Why You Need a Framework

A framework is simply a systematic way of doing your work that ensures consistent, quality results every time. Some entrepreneurs eventually turn their frameworks into products they sell—coaching programs, courses, or consulting services that teach others their proven methods. But even if you never plan to sell your framework as a course or coaching program, you still need one for yourself.

Let me give you an example of what happens when you don't have a framework. When I was working as a full-time journalist and pursuing my master's degree, I hired a company to clean my apartment. I assumed they would clean everything I considered necessary. But when they finished, I noticed they hadn't touched the baseboards, cobwebs, or food splatters on the refrigerator and walls. When I pointed these out, they went back and cleaned them, but it was clear they had just cleaned whatever they felt like cleaning, not what I expected from a professional cleaning service.

What they needed was a framework—a checklist like the one we used at Borders Books and Music when our cleaning crew came in. Every area had specific tasks listed and the cleaners had to check and initial each item to confirm it was done. Without that framework, their workers just did whatever seemed right to them in the moment.

Needless to say, I never hired that company again. Their lack of a systematic approach cost them a repeat customer and probably many others. Here's why you need a framework, even for something as straightforward as house cleaning:

Clarity in sales conversations: When prospects ask "How do you help people?" you can walk them through your specific process instead of giving vague answers about your skills.

Consistent results: A framework ensures you don't skip important steps or forget crucial elements when working with different clients.

Professional credibility: Having a systematic approach positions you as an expert who knows exactly what they're doing, not someone who's figuring it out as they go.

Easier pricing: When you can clearly articulate the value you provide at each step, it's easier to price your services appropriately.

Scalability: A framework makes it easier to train employees or contractors to deliver your services consistently.

Building Your Framework: The 3-Pillar Method

The most effective frameworks have 3-5 core pillars—major areas of focus that clients need to address to achieve their desired outcome. Here's how to identify yours:

Step 1: Define the transformation

Start with the end in mind. What specific transformation do you provide? Not what you do, but what result your clients get.

For example:

- "I help real estate agents go from being unknown in their market to being the go-to expert people think of when they need to buy or sell."

- "I help small restaurants go from struggling with empty tables to having consistent customers and predictable revenue."

- "I help busy moms go from feeling overwhelmed and out of shape to having energy and confidence."

Step 2: Identify the major obstacles

What are the 3-5 biggest things preventing your ideal clients from achieving that transformation on their own? These obstacles become your pillars.

Using the real estate example:

- Obstacle 1: They don't have a clear niche or unique value proposition

- Obstacle 2: They're not positioned as an expert in anything specific

- Obstacle 3: They're not creating content that attracts their ideal clients

Step 3: Create your pillars

Turn each obstacle into a positive pillar that addresses the problem:

- Pillar 1: Define Your Value-Driven Niche

- Pillar 2: Monetize Your Expertise

- Pillar 3: Create Attraction Content

Step 4: Break down each pillar

Under each pillar, identify the specific steps or sub-components needed to complete that area:

Pillar 1: Define Your Value-Driven Niche

- Step 1: Analyze your past successful transactions

- Step 2: Identify your ideal client avatar

- Step 3: Research your competition in that niche

- Step 4: Craft your unique value proposition

- Step 5: Test your positioning with real prospects

Pillar 2: Monetize Your Expertise

- Step 1: Identify your unique knowledge and experience

- Step 2: Create valuable lead magnets

- Step 3: Develop your signature presentation

- Step 4: Build strategic partnerships

- Step 5: Launch your referral system

Pillar 3: Create Attraction Content

- Step 1: Develop your content calendar

- Step 2: Create educational video series

- Step 3: Write valuable blog posts

- Step 4: Engage on social media platforms

- Step 5: Track and optimize your results

Step 5: Sequence the work

Determine the logical order for implementing your framework. Some pillars might be worked on simultaneously, others need to be completed in sequence.

Naming Your Framework

Give your framework a memorable name that communicates the transformation you provide. Some examples:

- "The Attraction Authority Blueprint" (for real estate agents)

- "The Profit-First Restaurant System" (for restaurant owners)

- "The Confident Mom Method" (for busy mothers)

The name should be:

- Easy to remember

- Clearly connected to the outcome

- Professional but not overly complicated

- Unique to your approach

NOTE: I actually created the "Attraction Authority Blueprint" framework myself for real estate agents, and I've provided it here as an example of how the process works—you'll need to develop your own framework specific to your industry and expertise.

Testing and Refining Your Framework

Your first version won't be perfect, and that's okay. Here's how to improve it:

Start with one client: Walk your first client through your framework step by step. Pay attention to what works, what doesn't, and where they get stuck.

Document everything: Keep detailed notes about what you actually do with each client, not just what you planned to do.

Ask for feedback: After completing each pillar, ask clients what was most valuable and what could be improved.

Track results: Measure the outcomes clients achieve at each stage of your framework.

Refine regularly: Update your framework based on real-world results and client feedback.

Communicating Your Framework to Prospects

Once you have your framework, use it in every sales conversation:

"Here's how I help [ideal clients] achieve [desired outcome]. My process has three main phases: [Pillar 1], [Pillar 2], and [Pillar 3]. In the first phase, we focus on [brief description]. Then we move to [brief description of pillar 2]. Finally, we [brief description of pillar 3]. Most clients see [specific result] by the end of the process."

This approach immediately positions you as someone who has a proven system, not just someone with general skills.

Your Framework Is Your Foundation

Remember, your framework isn't just a marketing tool—it's the foundation of how you serve clients excellently. It ensures you deliver consistent results while building your reputation as someone who knows exactly how to solve your clients' problems.

Take time to develop this properly. It's one of the most important investments you can make in your business, and it will serve you well as you grow and scale your services.

Your framework becomes part of your unique value proposition. It's what separates you from competitors who just offer generic services without a clear process for achieving results.

Use Appendix B: 90-Day Business Model Test Plan to validate your framework with real clients.

Month 1 Focus: The Only 3 Things That Matter Right Now

When you're starting a business, everything feels urgent and important. You need a website, business cards, social media accounts, email systems, accounting software, legal documents, and a hundred other things.

Here's the truth: most of that can wait.

In your first month, there are only three things that actually matter:

1. Find one person who needs what you offer and serve them exceptionally well.

Not ten people. Not a hundred people. One person. Focus all your energy on understanding their problem deeply and solving it completely. This will teach you more about your business than any course or book ever could.

2. Document what you learn so you can repeat and improve it.

As you serve your first client, pay attention to what you do, how you do it, and what results you get. Write it down. This becomes the foundation of your systems and processes.

Don't worry about creating perfect systems from the beginning. Just document what you actually do so you can refine it later. The goal is to capture your process so you can improve it and eventually teach it to others.

3. Ask for honest feedback and a referral.

When you've served your first client well, ask them two questions: "What could I have done better?" and "Who else do you know who might need this help?"

The feedback helps you improve. The referral gives you your second client. Both are more valuable than any marketing strategy you could implement in month one.

That's it. Three things. Everything else is a distraction from these fundamentals.

See Appendix A: Priority Matrix For Faith-Driven Entrepreneurs to help you focus on what matters most; and use Appendix C: Client Feedback Template to gather honest input from your first clients.

Essential Tools: What You Actually Need

Here's something that might surprise you: there are really only two things you need to do to <u>start</u> a business. First, handle whatever legal requirements apply to your situation—which might be as simple as filing paperwork with your state, or might not be required at all depending on your business structure. Second, find customers who need what you offer. That's it. Everything else is just details you can figure out as you go.

Then, once you've started your business, the business tool industry will try to convince you that you need dozens of software subscriptions, complicated systems, and expensive equipment to <u>run</u> a business. That's not true.

Here's what you actually need to start and run most service-based businesses:

Communication: A phone number and an email address. That's it. You can upgrade to fancy CRM systems later, but you can run a six-figure business with email and phone calls.

Payment Processing: A simple way to accept payments. PayPal, Stripe, or even Venmo will work to start. You don't need complicated invoicing systems until you have enough clients to justify them.

Basic Website: A simple one-page website that explains what you do, who you serve, and how to contact you. You can build this yourself using templates, or hire someone on Fiverr for $50. Don't spend months perfecting your website before you have clients.

File Storage: Google Drive or Dropbox to store and share files with clients. Free versions work fine when you're starting out.

Calendar Scheduling: Calendly or a similar tool to let clients book time with you without the back-and-forth email dance.

That's the complete list for most businesses. Everything else—fancy CRM systems, email marketing platforms, project management tools, accounting software—can be added later as your business grows and you understand what you actually need.

The goal is to start serving clients, not to build the perfect tech stack.

The Integrity Advantage: Marketing Without Feeling Slimy

One of the biggest obstacles faith-driven entrepreneurs face is marketing. We want to serve people, but we don't want to feel like we're being pushy or manipulative.

Here's the key: marketing isn't about convincing people to buy something they don't need. It's about helping people who already have a problem understand that you can solve it.

When you approach marketing from a service mindset instead of a sales mindset, everything changes.

Instead of asking "How can I get people to buy from me?" ask "How can I help people understand that I can solve their problem?"

Instead of focusing on features and benefits, focus on transformation. What will their life or business look like after you've helped them?

Instead of using high-pressure tactics, use high-value content. Teach people something useful, even if they never hire you. This builds trust and demonstrates your expertise.

I could write an entire book specifically on marketing with integrity (and maybe I will someday), but here's what this looks like in practice:

Content that serves: Write blog posts, create videos, or share social media content that actually helps your target audience solve problems, even if they never pay you. This positions you as someone who genuinely cares about their success.

Honest testimonials: When clients get results, ask them to share their experience in their own words. Real stories from real people are more powerful than any sales copy you could write.

Clear communication: Be upfront about what you do, how you do it, what it costs, and what results people can expect. Transparency builds trust faster than clever marketing tactics.

Referral relationships: Build relationships with other service providers who serve your ideal clients but don't compete with you. They can refer clients to you, and you can refer clients to them.

The integrity advantage is that people want to work with someone they trust. When you market with integrity, you attract clients who value what you do and are willing to pay fairly for it.

This is why integrity in business isn't just the right thing to do—it's the smart thing to do. As Proverbs 16:8 reminds us: "Better is a little with righteousness than great revenues without right." It's better to build a smaller business with integrity than a large business built on questionable practices. When you operate with righteousness, you sleep well at night, you attract clients who respect you, and you build something that can last for generations.

Emotional Preparation: What to Expect in Your First 90 Days

Starting a business is an emotional rollercoaster, even when you're doing everything right. Here's what to expect and how to handle it:

Week 1-2: Excitement and Terror

You'll feel excited about the possibilities and terrified about the unknowns. This is normal. The excitement will fuel your initial actions. The terror will try to talk you out of continuing. Expect both and don't let either one control your decisions.

Week 3-6: The Reality Check

Things will be harder than you expected. You'll realize you don't know as much as you thought you did. You'll make mistakes. You might start questioning whether you're cut out for this. This is also normal. Every successful entrepreneur goes through this phase. The ones who succeed are the ones who keep going anyway.

Week 7-12: The Breakthrough or the Breakdown

Around this time, you'll either start seeing real progress or you'll hit a wall that makes you want to quit. If you're seeing progress, celebrate it but don't get overconfident. If you're hitting a wall, remember that this is often right before the breakthrough happens. Most people quit during this phase, which is why most people don't succeed in business.

Spiritual Challenges You'll Face:

Doubt: You'll question whether God really called you to do this, especially when things get difficult. Remember that difficulty doesn't mean you're out of God's will. Sometimes it means you're exactly where He wants you to be.

Comparison: You'll see other entrepreneurs who seem to be doing better than you and wonder why your progress is slower. Remember that you're seeing their highlight reel, not their behind-the-scenes struggles. Focus on your own journey.

Impatience: You'll want results faster than they come. Remember that God's timing is perfect, even when it doesn't match your timeline. Use the waiting periods to develop skills and character.

Fear: You'll be afraid of failure, afraid of success, afraid of making the wrong decisions. Remember that "God hath not given us the spirit of fear; but of power, and of love, and of a sound mind." (2 Timothy 1:7, KJV)

When you're facing the emotional ups and downs of starting a business, remember that your strength doesn't come from your own confidence or abilities. Paul reminds us in Philippians 4:13: "I can do all things through Christ which strengtheneth me." This isn't a promise that everything will be easy, but it's a promise that you have access to supernatural strength for whatever God calls you to do. When clients reject you, when money gets tight, when you question whether you can really do this—that's when you lean into His strength, not your own.

How to Handle the Emotional Ups and Downs:

Daily Prayer: Start each day by committing your work to God and asking for His guidance. End each day by thanking Him for what He's taught you, even if the day didn't go as planned.

Weekly Review: Every week, write down what you learned, what worked, what didn't work, and what you'll do differently next week. This helps you see progress even when it doesn't feel like you're making any.

Monthly Celebration: At the end of each month, celebrate what you've accomplished, no matter how small. Starting a business is hard, and every step forward is worth acknowledging.

Find Your Tribe: Connect with other faith-driven entrepreneurs who understand what you're going through. This might be through online communities, local business groups, or your church. You need people who can encourage you when things get tough.

Building Your Support System: Finding Your Tribe

You can't build a successful business alone. You need people who believe in what you're doing, understand the challenges you're facing, and can offer wisdom when you need it.

Here's who you need in your corner:

A Mentor: Someone who has built a successful business and can guide you through the challenges you're facing. This doesn't have to be someone in your exact industry, but it should be someone whose character and business practices you respect.

Peer Entrepreneurs: Other business owners who are at a similar stage as you. You can learn from each other, encourage each other, and hold each other accountable.

Spiritual Advisors: Mature believers who can help you discern God's will for your business and keep you grounded in biblical principles. This might be your pastor, a small group leader, or a trusted friend who knows Scripture well.

Professional Support: An accountant, lawyer, or other professionals who can help you handle the technical aspects of running a business. You don't need to hire these people full-time, but you should know who to call when you need help.

Family Support: If you're married, your spouse needs to be on board with your business journey. If you have kids, they need to understand why you're working extra hours and how this will benefit the family long-term.

Where to Find These People:

Local Business Groups: Many cities have entrepreneur meetups, chamber of commerce events, or industry-specific groups where you can meet other business owners.

Online Communities: There are Facebook groups, LinkedIn communities, and other online spaces where faith-driven entrepreneurs connect and support each other.

Your Church: Look for other entrepreneurs in your church who might be willing to mentor you or connect with you as peers.

Professional Organizations: Industry associations often have local chapters where you can network with others in your field.

Conferences and Events: Business conferences, especially those focused on faith-driven entrepreneurship, are great places to meet like-minded people.

Remember, building your support system takes time. Don't expect to find all these people immediately. Start with one or two relationships and build from there.

The 90-Day Milestone

If you can make it through your first 90 days in business, you've accomplished something significant. Most people never start, and many of those who do start quit within the first few months.

By day 90, you should have:

- Served at least one client and gotten real feedback

- Learned what you're good at and what you need to improve

- Developed basic systems for delivering your service

- Built relationships with a few potential clients or referral sources

- Gained confidence that you can actually do this

You probably won't be profitable yet, and that's okay. You might not even have a clear picture of what your business will look like long-term, and that's okay too.

What matters is that you've started. You've moved from thinking about building something to actually building it. You've partnered with God in creating value for others.

That's not just a business milestone. It's a spiritual milestone. You've stepped into the calling God placed on your life, and you've trusted Him enough to take action even when you couldn't see the whole path.

The Daily Discipline of Building

Here's something most business courses won't tell you: you're not truly ready until you show up consistently.

Think about it this way—if you're a basketball player who only plays on weekends, are you ready for the NBA? Of course not. The same principle applies to your business. You can't build something meaningful by working on it only when you feel like it or when it's convenient.

Showing up consistently means more than just doing the work you're paid to do. In the beginning, before you even have clients, you've got to put in work to get clients. That means showing up to market yourself consistently. Showing up to network consistently. Showing up to create content, make calls, send emails, and do whatever else is needed to succeed.

This is where a lot of faith-driven entrepreneurs get tripped up. They think that if God has called them to build something, it should come easily. They pray for clients, then sit back and wait for the phone to ring. But Jacob didn't just pray for favor—he showed up every day to tend the flocks, study the breeding patterns, and implement his strategies.

The daily discipline of building isn't glamorous. It's sending that follow-up email even when you don't feel like it. It's creating content even when no one seems to be paying attention. It's making that networking call even when you're tired from your day job.

But here's what happens when you show up consistently: you become the person who's there when your potential clients are ready to make a decision. And that timing matters more than you might think.

Competitors as Collaborators

One of the biggest mistakes new entrepreneurs make is looking at everyone in their field as competition. This scarcity mindset will kill your business before it even gets started.

Here's the truth: in the early stages of your business, other people doing what you do aren't taking customers away from you—they're proving that a market exists for your services. They should be your allies, not your enemies.

You should be trying to build relationships with them. Network with them. Learn from them. Many established business owners are willing to share insights with newcomers who approach them with respect and genuine interest in learning.

The ones who might see you as competition are usually the ones who are insecure about their own position. But established professionals understand something important: their brand, their personality, their unique approach, and their story are what attract their ideal clients. That's going to be different from how you do things.

Your real competition isn't other service providers. Your real competition is indecision.

Most people take a long time to make purchasing decisions, especially for services. They know they need help, but they procrastinate, research endlessly, or convince themselves they can figure it out on their own. Often, they finally decide to take action when they reach a breaking point—when they can't put off solving their problem any longer.

That's why consistency and follow-up are so crucial. You need to be the one who's there, providing value and staying in touch, when they finally reach that decision point. The business often goes to whoever delivered the last helpful message before the prospect decided they couldn't wait any longer.

This is why building relationships with others in your field is smart business. They might refer clients to you who aren't a good fit for them. You might collaborate on larger projects. You might learn strategies that help you serve your own clients better.

Approach your industry with an abundance mindset. There's enough work for everyone who's willing to show up consistently and serve people well.

Moving Forward with Confidence

Starting a business as a faith-driven entrepreneur isn't just about making money or achieving financial freedom. It's about stewardship. It's about using the gifts God gave you to serve others and create value in the world.

It's about building something that honors Him and provides for the people you love. It's about breaking cycles and creating new patterns for the generations that come after you.

The faithful starter strategy isn't about having perfect faith or perfect plans. It's about having enough faith to take the next step and trusting God to guide you as you go.

You don't need to see the whole staircase to take the first step. You just need to take the first step with confidence that God will light the way.

In the next chapter, we'll talk about how your business becomes more than just a way to make money—it becomes a ministry that serves God's purposes in the world.

But first, you need to start. Not next month, not when you're more prepared, not when you have more certainty.

Today.

Take the first step. Serve the first person. Build the first system. Make the first call.

God is waiting to partner with you in building something beautiful. But He can't bless what you never start.

Your business journey begins with a single step of faith. Take it.

THE FAITHFUL STARTER STRATEGY—ACTION CHECKLIST

- Framework Creation

  - Define the specific transformation you provide clients

  - Identify 3-5 major obstacles your clients face

  - Create pillars that address each obstacle

  - Break down each pillar into actionable steps

  - Name your framework memorably

  - Test with first client and refine based on results

- Month 1 Essentials

- ○ Find ONE person who needs what you offer

- ○ Serve them exceptionally well and document the process

- ○ Ask for honest feedback on your service

- ○ Request a referral to their network

- ○ Focus only on these activities—ignore everything else

- Essential Tools Setup

    - ○ Set up basic communication (phone/email)

    - ○ Choose simple payment processing method

    - ○ Create one-page website explaining what you do

    - ○ Set up file storage and sharing system

    - ○ Install calendar scheduling tool

- Integrity Marketing Plan

    - ○ Write content that serves your audience (even if they don't hire you)

    - ○ Collect honest testimonials from satisfied clients

    - ○ Be transparent about pricing and realistic expectations

    - ○ Build relationships with complementary service providers

    - ○ Focus on transformation stories rather than features/benefits

- Support System Building

    - ○ Identify potential mentors in your industry

- Connect with 2-3 peer entrepreneurs at similar stage

- Find spiritual advisors who can provide biblical guidance

- Locate professional support (accountant, lawyer) for when needed

- Ensure family is supportive of your business journey

- Daily Discipline Implementation

  - Commit to showing up consistently every day

  - Create daily/weekly marketing activities schedule

  - Set up follow-up systems for prospects

  - Build relationships with others in your field (not competitors, collaborators)

  - Track your activities and results weekly

8

YOUR BUSINESS IS YOUR MINISTRY

Building something that honors God and serves people

I was sitting in my client's office reviewing her social media content when she said something that caught me completely off guard.

"You know, the copy you've been writing makes me sound so good that I'm actually intimidated. I'm not sure I can live up to how you're making me sound."

She'd been in her industry for over 25 years and was thinking about winding down her practice. But then she said something that surprised me even more.

"At the same time, reading what you wrote has motivated me to want to do more. I've been thinking about slowing down, but this makes me want to work harder, to actually become the person you're describing in this content."

A few weeks later, during another meeting, she brought up something she'd been thinking about. She follows a couple of different churches and loves their sermons, and she was considering sharing some of their faith-based content on her Facebook business page instead of her personal page, where she doesn't spend much time and has fewer connections.

"I think it might encourage some people who don't attend a good Bible-based church," she explained. "And I figure my patients who are believers would get encouragement from it. But I'm wondering—as my marketer, do you think this might hurt my business?"

I told her that as long as it aligned with her brand, she should absolutely incorporate more faith-based content. Then I offered to create that kind of content for her on a regular basis. She was ecstatic and said she would love to do that more regularly.

That's when it hit me: this wasn't just business. This was ministry.

Not only was I helping her present her best self to the world and motivating her to grow in her calling, but I was also helping her share messages of faith with her audience. I was serving others in a way that reflected God's character and advanced His purposes in the world.

Your business isn't separate from your calling. It IS your calling.

Let Your Light Shine

Your business isn't just about making money or achieving personal success—it's about being a light in the marketplace. Jesus said in Matthew 5:16: "Let your light so shine before men, that they may see your good works, and glorify your Father which is in heaven."

When you operate with integrity, serve your clients excellently, and treat your competitors with respect, you're not just building a business—you're demonstrating God's character to a watching world. Your business becomes a testimony that points people to Him.

This doesn't mean you need to quote Scripture in every sales meeting or put Bible verses on your business cards. It means that the way you conduct business should be so different, so excellent, so genuinely caring that people notice something unique about you.

It means being honest about what your services can and cannot do. It means delivering more value than you promised. It means treating your employees, vendors, and even difficult customers with dignity and respect.

It means building something that would make God proud to have His name associated with it.

Serving Clients as Unto the Lord

"And whatsoever ye do, do it heartily, as to the Lord, and not unto men." (Colossians 3:23, KJV) This verse transforms how you approach every aspect of your business. When you serve clients as unto the Lord, you're not just trying to satisfy a customer—you're offering your work as worship to God.

What does this look like practically?

Excellence becomes your standard, not perfection. You do your best work not because you're trying to impress people, but because you're offering it to God. You don't cut corners or deliver subpar results because "it's good enough." You deliver excellence because that's what honoring God looks like.

Honesty becomes non-negotiable. You tell clients the truth about timelines, costs, and realistic expectations, even when the truth might cost you the sale. You admit when you've made mistakes and make them right quickly. You don't overpromise and underdeliver because your word reflects God's character.

Service becomes your motivation, not just profit. While you charge fairly for your work and expect to be profitable, your primary motivation is genuinely helping your clients succeed. You celebrate their wins as much as your own. You refer them to competitors when someone else would serve them better.

Patience becomes your response to difficult situations. When clients are unreasonable, when projects go sideways, when people don't pay on time, you respond with patience and grace rather than anger and retaliation. You understand that how you handle difficult situations often says more about your character than how you handle easy ones.

This doesn't mean being a pushover or accepting abuse. It means handling business challenges with the same character you'd want to display if Jesus were sitting in the room watching how you respond.

"If I then, your Lord and Master, have washed your feet; ye also ought to wash one another's feet. For I have given you an example, that ye should do as I have done for you." (John 13:14-15, KJV).

Jesus demonstrated the ultimate example of servant leadership. He showed us that true greatness comes from serving others, not being served. Your business gives you the opportunity to wash feet in the marketplace—to serve your clients with humility and excellence, putting their needs ahead of your ego.

The Boaz Legacy: How Righteous Business Decisions Ripple Through Generations

Remember Boaz from earlier in the book? His story shows us something powerful about how business decisions made with integrity can impact generations.

When Boaz chose to redeem Ruth's situation, he wasn't just helping a widow and her mother-in-law. He was making a business decision that would affect his own finances, his family's future, and his community's perception of him.

He could have declined. The responsibility was real, and so was the cost. Other men in his position might have found reasons to pass the responsibility to someone else or negotiate a better deal for themselves.

But Boaz chose to do the right thing, even when it was costly and complicated.

The result? Ruth and Boaz had a son named Obed. Obed became the father of Jesse. Jesse became the father of David. And from the house of David came Jesus, the Redeemer of the world.

A legal transaction. A marriage covenant. A family redeemed. And the lineage of Christ preserved, all from one righteous business decision.

This is the Boaz Legacy: righteous choices in business ripple through generations in ways we may never fully see or understand.

When you choose integrity over profit, when you serve others excellently even when it costs you, when you build something that honors God rather than just enriching yourself, you're not just affecting your immediate situation. You're creating ripples that will impact your children, your community, and people you'll never meet.

Your business decisions are never just business decisions. They're character decisions that shape who you become and what you leave behind.

Redefining Success Beyond Just Profit

The world measures business success primarily by financial metrics: revenue, profit margins, market share, growth rates. While these things matter and are important for sustainability, they're not the complete picture of success for a faith-driven entrepreneur.

Here's how to measure success when your business is your ministry:

Lives Changed: How many people are better off because of what you've built? This might be clients whose businesses are thriving because of your services, employees who've developed new skills working for you, or community members who've benefited from your success.

Character Developed: How has building this business shaped you into the person God wants you to be? Have you become more patient, more generous, more faithful? Have you learned to trust God in new ways?

Kingdom Impact: How is your business advancing God's purposes in the world? This might be through the direct service you provide, the way you treat people, the resources you're able to give to ministry, or the example you set for other believers.

Generational Influence: What kind of legacy are you creating for your children and their children? Are you modeling what it looks like to use your gifts in service to others? Are you building wealth that can bless future generations?

Personal Fulfillment: Are you using the gifts God gave you in ways that energize and fulfill you? Do you wake up excited about the work you get to do? Do you feel like you're living out your calling?

This doesn't mean financial success doesn't matter. Profitability is important because it allows you to continue serving others, provide for your family, and give generously to causes you care about. But it's not the only measure of success, and it's not the most important one.

Growing Without Burning Out

One of the biggest challenges faith-driven entrepreneurs face is learning how to grow their business without sacrificing their soul, their family, or their relationship with God.

The world tells you that success requires grinding 80-hour weeks, sacrificing everything for your business, and pushing through exhaustion to reach your goals. But that's not God's design for your life or your business.

Here's how to grow sustainably:

Remember the Sabbath principle. God designed you to work six days and rest one. This isn't just a suggestion—it's a commandment that reflects how He created you to function. Taking regular rest isn't lazy; it's obedient. It's also practical—you make better decisions, serve clients better, and avoid costly mistakes when you're well-rested.

Build systems, not dependencies. Instead of making yourself indispensable to every aspect of your business, create systems and train others to handle routine tasks. This allows you to focus on the high-value activities that only you can do while giving you margin for rest and family time.

Set boundaries and keep them. Decide what hours you'll work, what types of clients you'll serve, and what services you'll offer. Then stick to those decisions even when opportunities arise that tempt you to compromise. Boundaries aren't limitations—they're the framework that allows you to serve excellently within sustainable parameters.

Delegate and trust others. As your business grows, you'll need to hire employees or contractors to help you serve more people. This requires learning to trust others with tasks you could do yourself. It's often harder and more expensive in the short term, but it's essential for long-term growth and sustainability.

Measure what matters most. If you only measure revenue and profit, you'll optimize for those things even at the expense of your health, relationships, and character. Also measure things like time with family, energy levels, client satisfaction, and personal growth. What gets measured gets managed.

Stay connected to your why. When business gets stressful, it's easy to lose sight of why you started in the first place. Regularly remind yourself of the people you're serving, the problems you're solving, and the calling God placed on your life. This helps you make decisions based on purpose rather than just pressure.

Growing without burning out isn't about working less—it's about working more strategically and sustainably. It's about building something that serves others well while also serving the life God has called you to live.

Creating a Legacy That Matters

At the end of your life, what do you want people to say about the business you built?

Do you want them to remember how much money you made, or how many lives you changed?

Do you want them to talk about your market share, or your character?

Do you want them to focus on your achievements, or your impact?

The legacy you leave isn't determined by the size of your business or the amount of wealth you accumulate. It's determined by how you used what God gave you to serve others and advance His purposes in the world.

A legacy that matters is built through:

Faithful stewardship of your gifts. Using your talents, skills, and opportunities to create value for others rather than just accumulating wealth for yourself.

Integrity in all your dealings. Building a reputation for honesty, fairness, and excellence that opens doors for other believers in business.

Generosity with your success. Using the resources your business generates to bless others, support ministry, and meet needs in your community.

Mentorship of the next generation. Teaching others what you've learned, helping them avoid your mistakes, and giving them the guidance you wish you'd had when you started.

Investment in eternal things. Building something that has impact beyond your lifetime—whether that's through the people you've served, the employees you've developed, or the resources you've provided for kingdom work.

Your business is temporary. Your legacy is eternal.

The question isn't whether you'll leave a legacy—everyone does. The question is what kind of legacy you'll leave.

Marketplace Ministry

Here's something most Christians don't understand: the marketplace is one of the most important mission fields in the world.

Think about it. Where do people spend most of their waking hours? At work or dealing with businesses. Where do they make decisions that affect their families, their futures, and their communities? In the marketplace. Where do they experience stress, hope, disappointment, and success on a daily basis? In their economic lives.

When you build a business that operates according to biblical principles, you're not just making money—you're demonstrating what the kingdom of God looks like in practical, everyday situations.

You're showing people what it looks like when someone keeps their word, delivers excellent service, treats employees with dignity, and cares more about serving than selling.

You're proving that you can be successful without compromising your integrity, that you can be profitable while being generous, and that you can build wealth while blessing others.

You're creating an environment where people can experience grace, excellence, and genuine care in the middle of their ordinary business day.

This is ministry. It's not preaching from a pulpit, but it's proclaiming the gospel through your actions, your character, and your commitment to serving others well.

The marketplace needs more believers who understand that their business is their ministry. It needs people who will demonstrate God's character through how they conduct commerce, treat employees, and serve customers.

It needs you.

Your Calling, Your Ministry, Your Legacy

As we come to the end of this book, I want you to understand something: the business you're called to build isn't just about you.

It's about the people you'll serve, the employees you'll develop, the community you'll impact, and the legacy you'll leave for future generations.

It's about demonstrating that faith and business not only can mix, but should mix. That believers can be successful in the marketplace while maintaining their integrity and advancing God's purposes.

It's about using the gifts God gave you to create value, solve problems, and make the world a little bit better than you found it.

The direction you needed is in these pages. The principles that will guide you are rooted in Scripture. The examples of others who've walked this path successfully are all around you.

What you need now is the courage to start.

To take the first step of faith into the calling God has placed on your life.

To stop feeling guilty about wanting to build something meaningful and start building it.

To transform your gifts into service, your service into business, and your business into ministry.

The world is waiting for what you have to offer. Your community needs the solution you can provide. Your family needs the provision and flexibility that business ownership can create.

And you need the fulfillment that comes from using your gifts in partnership with God to serve others and advance His kingdom.

Your business is your ministry. Your ministry is your calling. Your calling is your legacy.

Go build something beautiful.

9

GO BUILD SOMETHING BEAUTIFUL

The miracle is waiting on your move

I had been anxious for years before I reconnected with God. I was scared I wasn't going to make it. Scared I was going to end up homeless or as a failure. I had read books and taken courses, but I wasn't following anyone's footsteps and didn't have a real blueprint for building my business.

All I really had was the inner voice of God instructing me what to do. At first, I didn't know it was God, so I didn't always listen. Plus, I was scared, so I didn't always trust Him or the process as I should have.

But here's what I've learned: you're not waiting on the miracle. The miracle is waiting on your move.

I can't remember where I first heard that phrase, but it resonated with me because it's true. God has already equipped you with everything you need to start. The gifts, the skills, the burden for certain people, the ideas that won't leave you alone—that's all Him preparing you for what's next.

God Is an Entrepreneur

Think about it: God's creation of us, the universe, and everything in it is entrepreneurial work. He saw problems (darkness, emptiness, loneliness) and created solutions (light, earth, humanity). He built something from nothing, established systems that work, and continues to manage and grow His creation.

When you start a business, you're reflecting His creative nature. You're participating in His ongoing work of bringing order from chaos, solutions from problems, and value from raw materials.

This isn't separate from your spiritual life—it IS your spiritual life.

When God Gives You Ideas

When you get a business idea and you get excited about it, that's often God talking to you. Don't dismiss those moments of inspiration as just wishful thinking.

You might not be in a position to pull off that exact idea right now. Your current circumstances might require you to start with one type of business and work your way up to the bigger vision—which is exactly what I'm doing with my marketing agency positioning me to eventually build my film production company. But be in tune with your intuition. Pay attention to what excites you and won't let you go.

And remember this: if you get excited about an idea because God gave it to you, but then later you get doubt that it'll work, that doubt usually isn't from God—it's Satan trying to make you doubt yourself.

God doesn't give you doubt. He gives you vision, then equips you to fulfill it.

There are realities in the world that might require you to accomplish some smaller goals before you reach your bigger goal. But the doubt that tells you it's impossible? That's not from Him.

Control Your Own Evolution

Here's another advantage of building your own business that most people don't consider: it protects you from being replaced by emerging technologies.

As an employee, someone else decides whether new technology enhances your role or eliminates it—and whether the company adapts fast enough to stay competitive. You're vulnerable to decisions completely outside your control.

When you own a business, you control how technology affects your work. You control how quickly you adapt, which technologies you implement, and how you use them to better serve your customers. You're not waiting for permission to innovate—you're leading the innovation in your market.

It Will Take Longer Than You Think

Always keep in mind: building a business will take longer than you think it will, but that doesn't mean you're not making progress.

When I was a journalist, I was respected and known by a lot of people in my field. But that didn't immediately transfer into clients for my marketing business because that's not what I was known for. I had to consistently show up to prove that I was a marketer.

I'm sure people were thinking, "If you're so good at marketing, why don't you have more clients?" The truth is, in the beginning, I was still figuring out my target market and my offer. I took on clients who ultimately taught me what type of clients I didn't want. I once worked with a dance troupe that had gone viral, but the relationship didn't work because I couldn't travel with them to create original content, and they were too busy to implement the strategies I recommended. It wasn't anyone's fault—it just wasn't a good fit.

Those experiences weren't failures. They were education. They taught me who I could serve best and how to structure my services for success.

"He that is faithful in that which is least is faithful also in much." (Luke 16:10, KJV)

Be faithful in the small matters, the early clients, the imperfect situations. God is preparing you for greater things through every experience.

You're Not Retiring from God's Work

Here's something I need to address: I don't agree with the traditional concept of retirement. In fact, I don't see retirement anywhere in the Scriptures. There's no biblical precedent for stopping your productive work at a certain age and living off accumulated wealth while contributing nothing to God's kingdom. Moses was leading Israel at 120, Caleb was conquering mountains at 85, and Anna was serving in the temple well into her advanced years.

I don't believe God wants you to rest on your laurels at age 65 and stop contributing to His kingdom. You'll have plenty of time to rest when you pass away.

Now, don't misunderstand me—you need to take the Sabbath, and you need to rest when your body tells you to rest. But this idea of "I'm going to retire and sit on a beach for the next 15 years doing nothing" doesn't align with biblical stewardship.

Why would you ever retire from God's work?

If you want to switch careers, fine. If you want to change how you serve, that makes sense. But to completely stop using your gifts to help others? That's burying your talents.

Plus, many people who think they have enough money to retire discover they don't when inflation and unexpected expenses hit. You never know what economic changes are coming.

Instead of planning to retire, plan to keep serving in different ways as you age. Your business can provide the flexibility to work less while still contributing meaningfully to God's kingdom.

Your Ripple Effect

"Thou shalt love thy neighbour as thyself." (Matthew 22:39, KJV)

If you don't genuinely care about the people you serve, they won't want to do business with you. But when you love your neighbors as yourself, when you treat their success as important as your own, business becomes a natural expression of that love.

You can't change the whole world by yourself, but if you can touch enough people, you can create a chain reaction. Every client you serve excellently tells others about their experience. Every employee you develop goes on to impact other organizations. Every principle you demonstrate in the marketplace influences other business owners to operate with more integrity.

Remember that by your example, other people start to think about the Lord. You are the light in your marketplace, whether you realize it or not.

The knowledge and skills you've gained in life are blessings meant to be shared with others. You have an obligation to use them to help uplift others.

Step Off the Ledge

There's a story about the apostle Paul that illustrates something important about faith and action. Paul wasn't known as a great speaker—in fact, his peers sometimes criticized his speaking ability. But he had to step off the ledge to discover how well he could fly.

You might not feel ready. You might not have all the skills you think you need. You might be worried about what others will think.

But sometimes you have to step off the ledge to discover what God can do through you.

The business you're called to build is waiting for you to take that first step of faith. Not when you're perfectly prepared, not when you have all the answers, not when the conditions are ideal.

Now.

God didn't design you for stagnation. He calls us to continual growth, ongoing sanctification, and forward movement throughout our entire lives. Your business is part of that journey—a way to keep growing, serving, and becoming more like Christ through the challenges and opportunities He places before you.

A Final Prayer

Heavenly Father, I pray for the person reading these words who feels the stirring in their heart to build something meaningful. Give them courage to step past their fears and into their calling. Show them clearly what You want them to build and who You want them to serve.

Provide them with the resources, the relationships, and the wisdom they need to succeed. Help them remember that their business is not separate from their faith, but an expression of it.

Bless the work of their hands. Multiply their efforts. Use their businesses to demonstrate Your character in the marketplace and to advance Your kingdom in practical, everyday ways.

And when they face challenges, remind them that they're not building alone. You are their partner, their provider, and their source of strength.

In Jesus' name, Amen.

APPENDIX A: PRIORITY MATRIX FOR FAITH-DRIVEN ENTREPRENEURS

Use this system to prioritize every task, decision, and opportunity in your business. Assign each item a letter based on importance and urgency:

A = Critical & Urgent (Do First—Complete within 1-2 weeks)

- Legal/safety requirements that could shut down your business

- Client deliverables with firm deadlines

- Cash flow emergencies or payment issues

Examples: Deliver promised work to paying client, handle customer complaint, file required business paperwork

B = Important But Not Urgent (Schedule—Complete within 1-2 months)

- Activities that build long-term business success

- Skill development that improves your service quality

- Marketing activities that generate future clients

- System building that creates efficiency

Examples: Create your service framework, build your website, develop marketing content, network with potential referral partners

C = Nice To Have (Delegate or Do Later—Complete within 3-6 months)

- Tasks that might help but aren't essential for success

- Activities that perfect rather than improve your business

- Low-impact marketing or administrative tasks

Examples: Perfect your logo design, organize your filing system, attend non-essential networking events, optimize minor website details

D = Eliminate (Don't do at all—these are distractions)

- Activities that don't serve your business goals

- Perfectionism disguised as productivity

- Busy work that makes you feel productive but doesn't create results

Examples: Endless research without action, comparing yourself to competitors on social media, reorganizing things that already work fine

How To Use This System:

1. Daily Planning: Each morning, list your tasks and assign A, B, C, or D

2. Do all A tasks first: Never work on B tasks while A tasks remain undone

3. Schedule B tasks: Put these on your calendar with specific deadlines

4. Delegate or delay C tasks: Only do these after A and B tasks are complete

5. Eliminate D tasks immediately: Don't put these on any list

Special Considerations For Faith-Driven Entrepreneurs:

- Prayer and spiritual disciplines are always A tasks—your relationship with God fuels everything else

- Family commitments are typically A tasks—don't sacrifice relationships for business success

- Rest and Sabbath are B tasks minimum—sustainable success requires intentional rest

- Serving existing clients well is always A—reputation is everything in business

Sample Priority Matrix

TASK	PRIORITY	DEADLINE	ACTION
Deliver client project	A	This week	Do first
Daily prayer/Bible study	A	Daily	Do first
Follow up with 3 prospects	A	This week	Do first
Create service framework	B	Next month	Schedule
Build email list	B	Next month	Schedule
Perfect website colors	C	When time allows	Delay
Research 10 more competitors	D	Never	Eliminate

Weekly Review Questions:

- What A tasks did I complete this week?

- What B tasks can I schedule for next week?

- What C tasks am I treating like A tasks?

- What D tasks am I wasting time on?

- How can I eliminate more D tasks next week?

Remember: You can do anything, but you can't do everything. This system helps you focus on what matters most for building a sustainable, God-honoring business.

APPENDIX B: 90-DAY BUSINESS MODEL TEST PLAN

Before you quit your job or invest significant money into a business idea, test it on a smaller scale first. This 90-day plan helps you gather real data about your business concept while minimizing risk.

Business Idea Being Tested:

Target Outcome:

Week 1-2: Setup & Preparation

- Define exactly what service/product you'll offer

- Identify 10 potential test clients/customers

- Create basic materials needed (simple website, business cards, etc.)

- Set up payment processing and basic systems

- Establish success metrics (number of clients, revenue, feedback scores)

Week 3-6: Initial Outreach

- Contact first 5 potential clients

- Follow up with prospects who didn't respond initially (most sales happen after multiple touchpoints)

- Offer free or heavily discounted service in exchange for detailed feedback

- Deliver service and document everything you do

- Track time spent on each aspect of the business

- Note what you enjoy vs. what drains you

Week 7-10: Refinement

- Contact next 5 potential clients

- Implement lessons learned from first group

- Begin charging closer to market rates

- Refine your service delivery process

- Start building referral relationships

Week 11-12: Evaluation

- Analyze all data collected

- Calculate actual hourly earnings

- Assess market demand and competition

- Evaluate personal satisfaction and energy levels

- Make go/no-go decision for full business launch

Weekly Tracking Sheet

Week	Hours Worked	Revenue Generated	Clients Served	Energy Level (1-10)	Key Learnings
1					
2					
3					
4					
5					
6					
7					
8					
9					
10					
11					
12					

APPENDIX C: CLIENT FEEDBACK TEMPLATE

Getting honest feedback from your early clients is crucial for refining your services and building credibility. This template helps you gather specific actionable insights while positioning yourself as a professional who cares about continuous improvement. Send this to each test client after completing their project:

Thank you for allowing me to serve you with [specific service provided]. As I continue to refine and improve my services, your honest feedback is invaluable.

Please answer these questions:

1. *What specific results did you achieve from working with me?*

2. *What was most valuable about my service?*

3. *What could I have done better or differently?*

4. *Would you hire me again for similar projects at full market rates?*

5. *Would you refer me to others who need this service?*

6. *On a scale of 1-10, how likely are you to recommend my services?*

7. *Any other feedback or suggestions?*

APPENDIX D: 90-DAY DECISION MATRIX

Use the criteria in this decision matrix to objectively evaluate whether to move forward with your business idea after completing your 90-day test.

CRITERIA	SCORE (1-10)	WEIGHT	WEIGHTED SCORE
Market Demand (Did people want to buy?)		x3 =	
Personal Enjoyment (Did you like the work?)		x3 =	
Profitability (Can you make enough money?)		x2 =	
Scalability (Can you grow this business?)		x2 =	
Skill Match (Are you good at this?)		x2 =	
Time Requirements (Does this fit your life?)		x1 =	
Competition Level (Can you differentiate?)		x1 =	

Total Weighted Score: _______ / 140

Scoring Guide:

- 100-140: Strong business opportunity—proceed with confidence

- 70-99: Promising but needs refinement—test for another 30 days

- 40-69: Significant challenges—consider pivoting or trying different model

- Below 40: This business model isn't right for you—try something else

ABOUT THE AUTHOR

Penny Ray is an entrepreneur, marketer, and screenwriter who has spent decades learning what it means to build something meaningful from the ground up.

After serving four years in the United States Air Force, Penny discovered his talents for communication and entertainment, first as a nightclub DJ and then as a radio broadcaster. He became the number-one rated radio host in his market for his time slot, spending four years creating content, writing commercials, and handling audio production while dreaming of starting his own company.

Following his radio career, Penny transitioned into retail management with Borders Books and Music, managing stores in Virginia and Florida until the company's closure. This experience taught him valuable lessons about business operations and the importance of adapting to changing markets.

Determined to pursue his calling as a storyteller, Penny became a journalist, working for notable publications including *Homicide Watch D.C.*, *The Trentonian* in Trenton, New Jersey, and *The Cherokee Scout* in Murphy, North Carolina. During this time, he earned a bachelor's degree in journalism and a master's degree in professional screenwriting, all while working full-time.

Throughout his varied career path, Penny recognized that the skills he was developing—writing, communication, and storytelling—were exactly what businesses needed for effective marketing. Instead of waiting until he could fund his film projects to start a business, he launched a marketing agency, using his storytelling skills to help established businesses connect with their audiences.

Penny Ray

Today, Penny runs his marketing agency while continuing to develop his film production company. He writes screenplays, produces content, and helps other entrepreneurs discover and step into their God-given callings.

Penny lives in Western North Carolina.

Create Your Calling is his first book.